· LOCAL · FLAVOUR · SERIES ·

COOKING
&
LOOKING
in
CAIRNS
& DISTRICT

Compiled and
illustrated by

·Rosemary·
·Sinclair·

Edited by

·Joy·
·Hayes·

AYERS & JAMES HERITAGE BOOKS
Sydney 1986

Titles available in the
Local Flavour Series:

Cooking & Looking in Canberra
Cooking & Looking in Sydney's Rocks Area
Cooking & Looking in Cairns & District
Cooking & Looking in Fremantle

Illustrated by Rosemary Sinclair
Designed by Judy Hungerford
Project editing by Joy Hayes, Creative Pages
Project management by Book Production Services Pty Ltd
Typeset and assembled by Rochester Photosetting Service
Printed in Singapore

ISBN 0 949256 04 8

* C·O·N·T·E·N·T·S *

ON MEASUREMENTS

Trying new recipes has long been one of my favourite pastimes, and because the major difficulty encountered has been working out stipulated measurements, I've tried to make the recipes easy for everybody to follow.

Keeping in mind that cooking is an art, *not* a science, I've used cup measurements where practicable (i.e. ordinary tea-cup size not the little dainty one!). Otherwise, measurements are given in both the metric and imperial scales.

Some cooks believe it necessary to weigh everything, but I've never done so, and can't recall any failures as a result.

GENERAL MEASUREMENTS
FOR SCALE-SCORNING COOKS

1 breakfast cup sieved flour, lightly filled	125 g	= 4 oz
1 breakfast cup liquid	250 ml	= ½ pt
2 breakfast cups solid butter	500 g	= 1 lb
2 breakfast cups granulated sugar	500 g	= 1 lb
2½ breakfast cups icing sugar	500 g	= 1 lb
1 tablespoon butter, rounded	60 g	= 2 oz
2 tablespoons flour, rounded	30 g	= 1 oz
2 tablespoons desiccated coconut (level)	30 g	= 1 oz
2 dessertspoons liquid (1 tablespoon)	20 ml	
2 teaspoons (1 dessertspoon)	10 ml	
4 teaspoons (1 tablespoon)	20 ml	
1 teaspoon	5 ml	

Note: North American readers need to remember that their tablespoon equals 15 ml or 3 teaspoons.

OVEN TEMPERATURES

It is difficult to advise exact oven temperatures as different makes of stoves give different results at the same temperature reading. Indeed, many fuel stoves still in use have no temperature gauge, and a degree of guesswork is unavoidable.

The following chart should be helpful for most stoves.

OVEN DESCRIPTION	TEMPERATURE GAUGE		
	Automatic Electric	*Gas*	*0°C (or Celsius)*
Cool	200	200	100
Very slow	250	250	120
Slow	300–325	300	150–160
Moderately slow	325–350	325	160–170
Moderate	350–375	350	170–190
Moderately hot	375–400	375	190–200
Hot	400–450	400	200–230
Very hot	450–500	450	230–260

* I·N·T·R·O·D·U·C·T·I·O·N *

The tropics have their effect! 'You've gone troppo!' was the laughing response to my complaints of lethargy and lack of interest in little else than relaxing in Cairns. What a wonderful way to feel, in the tropical luxury of far north Queensland. Mind you, there's plenty to do and see. With Cairns as their starting point, visitors are 'within *cooee*' of the Great Barrier Reef, the eighth wonder of the world; Green Island, with its safe, year-round swimming; the beauty and beaches of Mossman and Port Douglas to the north; Kuranda Railway and the Atherton Tablelands.

Cairns itself is the game fishing base which attracts anglers from all parts of Australia and the world. The Marlin Jetty's weighing scales have tipped over 500 kilograms on countless occasions.

While the city's history is comparatively brief, it is tinged with fascination, and there are tales aplenty of a multicultural community involved in gold mining and sugarcane farming, of wartime dramas and dangerous exploits.

Cairns developed only because a port was desperately needed as an outlet for the newly discovered Hodgkinson goldfield in 1816. Cooktown, already established to serve the Palmer goldfield, was too far away.

Trinity Bay was named by Captain Cook when he sailed through it in 1770. The inlet was later explored in 1873 by G. E. Dalrymple, who had reported favourably on its possibilities as a harbour. With this in mind, a party of three men, led by Bill Smith, set out from the Hodgkinson to cut a track through to the inlet — a distance they thought to be about fifty miles. They reached the top of the range overlooking the inlet before illness forced their return to the goldfield. A few months later they made a second attempt to find a track from the coast, this time via Cooktown and by boat to the inlet.

The government of the day also played its part by sending the Cardwell Police Magistrate, B. G. Sheridan, to explore Trinity Inlet, with a view to establishing a town at an appropriate site. He spent two weeks in the area and, according to a report by S. E. Stephens to the Cairns Historical Society, selected a site where Dalrymple had camped in 1873, naming it 'Thornton' after the Premier of Queensland, George Thorn. An official party was then sent from Townsville to Trinity Inlet to establish the new town and port. The party was headed by David Spence, R. J. Hartley, Captain Nylchreest and J. P. Sharkey.

On 7 October 1876 the new port was officially proclaimed and named 'Cairns' after Queensland's governor at the time, William Wellington Cairns.

Prior to the proclamation of Cairns on 7 October 1876, the settlement was variously known as Thornton, Dickson, Newport and Trinity Bay.

When the first official party arrived in Cairns from the *Porpoise* in October 1876, they landed on the beach at a spot adjacent to the Strand Hotel (now the site of Pacific International). At that time the whole of the waterfront was a dense mass of tangled vegetation. According to Mr John Miller, a member of the landing party, as he reported in 1926, it was 'the densest scrub you ever saw'. It enveloped all the area on which the city now stands.

The first 'buildings' were tents — as was the first Post Office. According to Mr Miller: 'We emptied a brandy case, cut the words "Cairns Post Office" on it with a penknife and hung the case on the corner of the tent.' The first street formed was from the beach to the site of the Pacific International and the second was Abbott Street.

While the mining field for which Cairns was established had only a brief period of prosperity, the town survived many setbacks and is now a large and prosperous city, with a population in 1985 of about 60 000. With the growth of the district as a tourist centre there is an ever-increasing flow of visitors. When the first Boeing 747 arrived at the new international terminal in 1984 a visitor was heard to say: 'Well here's Cannes! Where's the Film Festival?'

Visitors come from all over the world and include many United States' ex-servicemen who, during World War II, were among the two million American troops stationed in the region.

Restaurants offer a wide variety of foods representing the multicultural nature of the north, with a natural emphasis on local products, particularly seafood and fruit. No one could visit Cairns

Dr. Koch's memorial was erected by the people of Cairns to honour their first doctor, best known for his investigations into the cause of tropical fevers.

without sampling barramundi or coral trout, fresh and cooked straight from the sea, or the famous Queensland mud crabs, sometimes so large they can take an hour to plough through. Such tasty fruits of the sea are positively addictive, as also are the tropical fruits like pineapples, pawpaws, mangoes, bananas, passionfruit, avocados and more exotic varieties of kiwi fruit, mangosteens and star-fruit.

One aspect of tropical north Queensland about which prospective tourists need advice, is the wet season. It can teem down in buckets every day between January and March. While unsuspecting travellers feel the necessity for webbed feet, the season is greeted happily enough by locals. 'Greening time', I was smilingly advised as the shoes were emptied!

While Cairns itself offers everything for visitors, it is also the starting point for the discovery and enjoyment of so much more of this delightful part of Australia. With its international airport opened in March 1984, Cairns is truly Australia's Northern Gateway.

The kindness and generosity of north Queenslanders enhanced the enjoyment of my task in preparing this book and I am most grateful to all who assisted in the acquisition of material. Special thanks to the *Cairns Post*, Cairns Municipal Library, Cairns City Council, Mulgrave Shire Council, Game Fishing Club, Pacific International Hotel, Cairns Historical Society, Graham Knell and Co. (solicitors), Lenore Knell, Don and Leslie Fry, Betty Vievers, Eileen Fisk, Terry Boland, Tom Doherty, Mr and Mrs Rolfe Gelling, Mr and Mrs Jock Izatt, Mrs Stillman, Regina Robson, Gail Guidice and Dianna Bowden.

Thanks also to Northern Heritage Restaurant, House on the Hill, Tawny's Restaurant, Fathoms Restaurant, Barnacle Bill's Restaurant, Freshwater Connection (Great Northern Railroad Company), Nautilus Restaurant, Verandah's Restaurant, High Falls Farm, Rafferty's Restaurant (Abbott Manor), Hides Hotel, Chris Souhijaerte, Vic Piccone, Lady Joy Williams, Mrs Erin Davis, Gail Svanetti, Angela Capitanis, Barbara Gurst, Dale Rogers, Joan Croker, Bev Spilsbury, Mary Ann Evans, Wendy Grimley, Caroline Clarke, Dorothy Cannon, Merle Butland, Mary Meoli, Gay Bavinton, Joyce Jorgensen, Mrs A. Secombe, V. Dangaard, B. Woodhouse, Susan March, Dawn Busby, Lorraine Vallely, Judy Todd, Shirley Mackenzie, Jean Watkins, Laurel Eden, Marcia Walters, Catherine Lucas, Ronwyn Corcoran, Lois Holland, Monika Young, Mrs J. Ivanoc, Judy Schwenke, Joan Watkins, Paul Musk and Phil and Yvonne Barber.

* F·I·R·S·T C·O·U·R·S·E·S *

Avocados grow in glorious abundance in the Cairns district so this section has a predominance of recipes using this delicious tropical fruit.

AVOCADO AND CRAB

Mix together and chill:
200 g (6 oz) crab meat
1 cup finely chopped celery
½ teaspoon salt
185 ml (⅔ cup) mayonnaise
Cut *3 avocados* in halves, remove stones and sprinkle with *lemon juice*.
Fill halves with the chilled mixture and serve on a *bed of lettuce*.
Serves 6.

ROBYN'S CRAB AND CORN SOUP

This easy recipe is for those who are denied fresh Queensland mud crabs! It is quite delicious.
Mix in a saucepan:
1 large can creamed corn
1 can cream of chicken soup
1 can good quality crab meat, cartilage removed
1 soup can fresh milk
Heat to boiling point and let simmer 10 minutes. Serve sprinkled with *fresh chopped herbs* of your choice.
Serves 4.

AVOCADO FONDUE

Melt 125 g (4 oz) *butter* in a fondue pot, add 1 *small onion*, chopped, and saute gently until soft. Sift in ½ *cup flour* and cook for 2–3 minutes.

Remove from heat and add:
1 *cup milk*
½ *cup cream*
salt and pepper
4 *tablespoons lemon juice*
1 *cup mashed avocado*

Stir well, cook for five minutes, stirring constantly. Do not allow to boil.

Add ½ *cup grated cheese* and stir until melted. Blend in *brandy* to taste.

Dip peeled *cooked prawns* into avocado fondue and serve *brown bread and butter* separately.

COCKTAIL MUSHROOMS

Cut the stems from the required number of *button mushrooms*. Mix some *butter* and *chopped parsley* and add *garlic* to taste (optional). Put mushrooms open side up on an ovenproof dish and fill each one with a knob of parsley butter.

Place in a 150°–170°C (300°–325°F) oven until butter has melted and mushrooms are slightly browned.

May be served as a cocktail snack or as a vegetable.

AVOCADOS WITH SCRAMBLED EGGS

Halve 2 *large avocados* and brush with *lemon juice*. Set in a shallow pan containing *hot water* about 5 mm (¼ in) deep. Heat in a moderate oven 180°C (350°F) 5–10 minutes. *Do not overheat,* because this makes the avocados bitter.

Meanwhile, beat 6 *eggs* with ½ *cup milk or cream*, ½ *teaspoon worcestershire sauce* and *salt and pepper*.

Melt 30 g (1 oz) *butter*, add eggs and stir until softly scrambled. Spoon into warmed avocado shells, top with 4 *rashers bacon*, cooked and crumbled, and serve at once.

Serves 4.

HIGH FALLS FARM

In the cool fresh air of Whyanbeel Valley northwest of Mossman, visitors can enjoy the freshest farm products .

High Falls Farm, run by Ron and Rhonda Berry, has been opened to the public since May 1984 and is the first farm in Australia to grow plantains commercially. Plantains are a type of banana used extensively in the West Indies and Pacific Islands as a vegetable. At High Falls Farm they are used in a wide variety of delicious dishes in grills, on fish, as fritters or in fruit salads.

The blackboard menu also offers freshly picked vegetables and fruits and unusual dishes include sweet potato savoury omelet and pawpaw scones.

Rhonda expresses surprise that so many visitors find their fare unusual. She says, 'We just utilise our farm products.'

It is done so well that visitors keep coming back for more.

The following recipe comes from High Falls Farm whose other recipes in this book can be located from the index.

PLANTAIN AND BACON OPEN GRILL

Toast one side of as many *thick slices of bread* as desired. *Butter* the untoasted side. On each slice place the following layers:
plantain slices to cover
chopped shallot
1 piece of bacon
cheese slices to cover
Sprinkle with *sesame seeds*.
Place under grill to melt cheese. Serve with or without *salad*.

SWEET POTATO OMELET

Beat *3 eggs* with *1 dessertspoon water* and *salt and pepper*. Add *1 tablespoon grated cheese*.

Melt about *1 tablespoon butter* in a pan and add *4–5 slices boiled cold sweet potato*, turning them on both sides.

Add chopped *shallot*, turn up heat and add the egg mixture. Using a fork, bring eggs from side of pan to centre, until all liquid runs under. While centre is still creamy (but not runny), fold in halves.

Serve immediately with *salad* if desired.

Serves 2.

VERANDAH'S RESTAURANT

Verandah's, in 1985 voted Queensland's top restaurant, is very pretty and typically tropical, decorated in pinks and white with bamboo and lots of lush greenery. Tables are covered in a Raffles-style print with salmon overlays. There is a well-stocked attractive bar area — a feature of which is Verandah's 'Tropical Cocktail'.

Tony and Barbara Roach, the owners, opened for business in May 1984, with Stephen Gee their innovative chef. Stephen comes from England where he gained valuable experience at various restaurants and hotels, including being executive *sous chef* of the Holiday Inn in Plymouth and chef of the Astor Hotel.

He says, 'In the kitchen of Verandah's we cook in a mixture of modern and classical with a touch of Asian.' He is assisted by two other chefs.

When I ate there with friends the food was unsurpassed in its excellence.

The following recipe was contributed by Stephen Gee and other recipes from Verandah's Restaurant can be located through the index at the back of this book.

AVOCADO MOUSSE WITH TIGER PRAWNS

Cut 2 *avocados* in half, remove stone, scoop out flesh into a bowl. Add and liquidise:
2 tablespoons *lemon juice*
salt and pepper
Add:
1 tablespoon *chopped shallots*
1 *clove garlic*, crushed
4 tablespoons *mayonnaise*
Sprinkle 15 g (½ oz) *gelatine* over ½ cup *water*, allow to stand for a few minutes, then dissolve over *hot water*. Add to avocado mixture.

Whip ½ cup *cream* until stiff, fold into mixture, add *a little worcestershire sauce* to taste, and pour into a mould. Chill to set. Turn out of mould and decorate with peeled *cooked tiger prawns* and *lemon wedges*.

Serves 4–6.

GREEN RAVIOLI OF SWEETBREADS WITH WILD MUSHROOM SAUCE

Make a green pasta by combining:
250 g (8 oz) plain flour
2½ eggs, beaten
1 teaspoon salt
1 tablespoon oil
250 g (8 oz) spinach, liquidised

Allow to rest for 1 hour.

Meanwhile, take *500 g (1 lb) lamb sweetbreads*, prepared by soaking in frequent changes of fresh water, and bring to the boil in *1 litre (2 pints) chicken or veal stock* and *2–3 tablespoons tarragon vinegar* for 2–3 minutes. Remove the sweetbreads and cool, reserving the liquid for the ravioli.

Divide the sweetbreads into nugget-sized pieces, removing the gristle, and leave to cool.

Roll out the pasta flat and thin, and make small ravioli with the sweetbreads. Boil in the existing stock, adding another 3 litres (6 pints), for approximately 10 minutes.

Serve with the following *sauce*.

Soak *a packet of dried cepes or morels* in a small quantity of *stock*. Cut them into small pieces after draining.

Melt *75 g (3 oz) butter* in a pan, add the mushrooms and some *pepper*, and fry slowly for ten minutes. Add *75 g (3 oz) each cream and sour cream* to the mushrooms and simmer lightly to thicken.

Drain the ravioli, add to sauce and toss together. Sprinkle with chopped *fresh parsley*.

Serves 4–6.

AVOCADO DIP

Beat *125 g (4 oz) cream cheese* until smooth and add:
1 avocado, peeled, stoned and mashed
60 g (2 oz) ground roasted peanuts
1 dessertspoon lemon juice
1 teaspoon finely chopped onion
salt and pepper

Mix thoroughly and chill.

Serve in a small bowl surrounded by *potato crisps or crackers*.

PACIFIC INTERNATIONAL HOTEL

Opened in 1984, this first-class hotel is already established as one of Queensland's finest. It is situated right on the waterfront, with expansive views of sea and city. Operated by the Kamsler family, its history is well recorded within the hotel's environs.

The Pacific International stands on the site of two former hotels — the Strand and the Pacific. The latter, built in 1924, was demolished in 1975. At the time the first Pacific was built, the Sydney *Daily Guardian* reported that Cairns was a town 'Blessed with a hotel every few yards so nobody need go thirsty'. Cairns boasted the highest consumption of alcohol per head in Australia, so it is no surprise that in 1925 a brewery was established there. Another journalist described Cairns as 'an immoral place with a population comprised of the worst characters of a dozen races'.

Many famous characters of the South Pacific patronised that first Pacific: Somerset Maugham, en route to Torres Strait; Joseph Conrad, sailor later turned writer, on his way to the Dutch East Indies; Errol Flynn, on his way to and from New Guinea; and General Douglas MacArthur, during preparations for the Battle of the Coral Sea.

The new Pacific International Hotel follows the tradition of attracting famous people, as did indeed the Kamslers' previously owned motel, Tradewinds. In 1981 that motel earned for brothers Paul and George Kamsler, the Federal Government sponsored Small Business Award for outstanding achievement.

With two sons also working in the Pacific Hotel management, it is truly a family concern, and guests are assured of a pleasant stay. Accommodation is first-class, restaurants provide excellent regional cuisine and furnishings throughout blend beautifully with the surrounds. There is extensive use of cane furniture and colourful fabrics.

Pacific Hotel staff is youthful and includes a cross-section of local community groups. A number of bi- and tri-lingual Australians, the children of immigrants, are employed and are naturally of great assistance to non-English speaking tourists. Torres Strait Islanders are generally excellent chefs and are employed in the hotel restaurants.

Catering manager, Mark Kamsler, is dedicated to the establishment of a regional cuisine — one which concentrates on

seafood, vegetables and fruit, including exotic varieties previously unknown but easily grown in north Queensland. There is a strong Asian influence in the area and this is reflected in the cuisine.

WATERFRONT RESTAURANT

Pacific International Hotel's main restaurant, the Waterfront, provides a browse through local history, as well as first-class fare.

There the diner can study sea-loving Joseph Conrad's master's certificate. Later to become a famous author, Conrad's first ship was the Australian barge *Otago*.

The walls of the restaurant are adorned with many historical photographs, but the dominating feature is a one-third scale model of the bow of *Decapolis*, a naval training vessel which in 1879 carried Cairns cedar logs to London. The captain, Skipper Almond, later became portmaster of the colony of Queensland. The impressive model was painstakingly constructed by F.W. Woodnut and Co. of Innisfail.

ENDEAVOUR RIVER MUD CRAB AND CORN SOUP

Included in the Pacific International's Waterfront Restaurant's special Cuisine of the Pacific menu, this dish is one of many offered as a tribute to the district's first immigrants — the Chinese, Malays, 'Manila Men', Japanese and South Sea Islanders who laboured on the goldfields and sugarcane plantations of tropical Queensland.

This soup, a goldfields favourite, was introduced by Chinese miners during the 1856 gold rush. Queensland mud crabs were then (as now) in abundant supply and corn was a staple commodity.

Combine in a saucepan:
1 x 425 g tin creamed sweet corn
7 bowls fresh chicken stock
salt and pepper
½ teaspoon monosodium glutamate
Thicken with a little cornflour, and before serving add:
1 cup fresh crab meat
some chopped shallots
1 soupspoon Lee Seng Heng fish sauce
Serves 6.

PACIFIC EGG ROLL

Mix together:
500 g (1 lb) minced lean pork
150 g (5 oz) minced prawn meat
50 g (1½ oz) water chestnuts
6 soaked dry Chinese mushrooms
100 g (3 oz) minced onion
Marinate in a mixture of 2 raw eggs, some cornflour, fish sauce and seasoning.
Make 4 thin omelets using 2 eggs and roll the meat mixture in the omelets. Steam for 30 minutes. Remove and deep fry before serving. Serve sliced.
Serves 4.

CRAYFISH BALLS

Beat *1 egg* and combine in a bowl with:
2 cups cooked and finely diced crayfish
1 cup breadcrumbs
2 tablespoons chopped parsley
1 small grated onion
1 teaspoon salt
pinch pepper
pinch nutmeg

Form mixture into balls, coat with *1 cup flour*, dip into *1 beaten egg* and dust with more flour.

Shallow fry the balls in *oil*, one layer at a time. Keep warm.

To make the sauce, brown *3 tablespoons flour* in the oil remaining in the pan. Add:
1 small onion, chopped
2 tablespoons tomato paste
1½ cups water
½ teaspoon salt

Let the mixture bubble for a few minutes.

Serve balls on a platter accompanied by sauce in dipping bowl.

AVOCADO LIME

This recipe is for two people — multiply the ingredients according to the size of the party.

Avocado should be ripe — firm but soft to touch. Cut in half and remove stone with knife. Take a thin slice off the bottom of each avocado so that it will sit flat on the plate.

The sauce

Squeeze *1 or 2 limes* into a small bowl, then blend in sufficient amount of *natural yoghurt (2–3 tablespoons)*, *1 teaspoon honey*, *crushed hazelnuts* and a *dash of gin*. Season to taste.

Place avocados on plate, fill with lime sauce. Garnish with a *sprig of parsley, lemon twist, and/or a tomato wedge*.

Serves 2.

BAKED AVOCADOS

Cut 5 *avocados* in half lengthwise, remove seed and scoop out a little flesh.

Mix the flesh with:
250 g (8 oz) *camembert cheese*
2 tablespoons *lemon juice*
1 *clove garlic*, crushed
2 tablespoons chopped *parsley* or 1 tablespoon dried *parsley*
few drops *tabasco sauce*

When mixed well, fill halved avocados.

Place in an ovenproof dish, sprinkle with *sesame seeds* and bake in a moderate oven 180°C (350°F) for 10–15 minutes.

Serves 8.

AVOCADO AND GRAPEFRUIT APPETISER

Use amounts according to the number of servings required.

Peel and slice *avocados* lengthwise and sprinkle with *lemon juice*, or leave in a bowl with seed from fruit to preserve colour.

Peel *a grapefruit*, making sure all white pith is removed. Cut segments away from membrane.

Arrange alternate slices of avocados and grapefruit on *lettuce leaf* around individual plates and in centre of each plate place a *small bowl of cream cheese*, softened with *cream* and seasoned with *salt* and *pepper*. Add a few chopped *macadamia nuts* if liked, and a sprig of *parsley* to decorate.

SAVOURY EGGS

Hard boil 6 *eggs* and while hot peel, cut in half, remove yolks into a small bowl and mash well.

Add:
2 tablespoons *butter*
1 tablespoon *cream* or *milk*
2 tablespoons finely chopped *anchovies*

Put mixture into a piping bag and fill eggs in a swirling design. Decorate with 2 slices of *gherkin* on each half, resembling butterfly wings.

Makes 12.

* F·I·S·H & S·E·A·F·O·O·D *

The ready availability of the fruits of the sea enhances the attraction of the Cairns district as indeed the recipes here enhance this book!

CORAL TROUT IN CHAMPAGNE

Melt *50 g (2 oz) butter* in a large shallow saucepan. Saute two large, finely chopped *shallots* until transparent. Add *100 g (3 oz) sliced button mushrooms* and cook until tender. Remove from pan with a slotted spoon and keep warm.

Add another *50 g butter* to pan and saute *4 fillets of coral trout*, each *150–170 g (5–6 oz)* until lightly coloured. Return the mushrooms and shallots to the pan with the trout and add *6 tablespoons fish stock* and *¾ cup champagne* (add more if necessary to barely cover the fillets). Season with *salt and pepper*.

Simmer gently for 5 minutes until tender, then transfer fillets to a heated serving dish.

Add *½ cup cream* to liquid in pan and simmer, without boiling, until cream is warmed through. Strain and return to pan.

Mix *1 tablespoon cornflour* with a little *water* to a smooth paste and add to sauce. Cook, stirring continuously, over very low heat until sauce is smooth.

When ready to serve pour in another *¾ cup champagne*. Stir and mix with sauce until warm. Pour over coral trout fillets and serve immediately.

Serves 4.

MARLIN JETTY

Long before the Game Fishing Club premises were built close by the Marlin Jetty in 1980, keen anglers were coming to Cairns in droves, including many famous fishermen. One of today's most famous is American actor, Lee Marvin.

The person given credit for putting the area on the sportsman's map for marlin was an American, George Bransford, who had been stationed in Cairns during World War II. He returned later and had a vessel built there — the *Sea Baby*. From this boat Bransford caught the first 500 kilogram marlin ever landed in Cairns waters. It was he who started the industry in a professional way.

In the early days, post-fishing entertainment fell to the lot of Jock and Margaret Izatt — Jock still holds the position of club president. Bob and Dolly Dyer were frequent visitors and greatly enjoyed the Cairns hospitality. Since Bob's death, Dolly has donated to the club all his Cairns fishing memorabilia, now proudly displayed in 'Bob Dyer's Corner'.

The Game Fishing Club offers a recreation area for club members and includes dining and bar areas. It also provides information on charter boats. Of the club's 640 members, about 400 are locals and the remainder are from interstate and overseas. The club boasts members in many countries including the United States, Britain, South America, Thailand, Singapore, Japan, Germany, France, Kenya and Guam. They are attracted by the black marlin and other large sport fish caught in the district.

In the 1981 season (from September to December) thirty-five marlin over five hundred kilograms were weighed; in 1982 nineteen went over that mark; and sixteen topped five hundred kilograms in the 1983 season. While large numbers are caught, only a comparative few are weighed in. The remainder are tagged and released. The marlin crew place a small plastic clip on the fin for scientific study and the fish are immediately freed.

The most abundant fishing waters are around Lizard Island.

World-class game boats are available for hire in the marlin season, complete with skipper and crew. Boats are also available at a reduced rate during the remainder of the year for light tackle sportsfishing.

ISLAND FISH STEW

In a large saucepan, slowly saute *1 onion* and *1 capsicum*, sliced, in *2 tablespoons oil* for 10 minutes. Add *a clove of crushed garlic* and cook a further 1–2 minutes.

Stir through:
1 cup chopped parsley
250 g (8 oz) chopped mushrooms
2 x 425 g (14 oz) cans whole tomatoes
1 cup dry white wine
1 cup water
Bring to boil and allow to simmer for about 5 minutes.

Add:
1 bayleaf
1 kg (2 lb) chopped fish fillets
250 g (8 oz) peeled green prawns
salt and pepper
Simmer gently for 7–10 minutes, garnish with *chopped parsley* and serve with *garlic bread* and a *crisp green salad*.
Serves 6–8.

CORAL TROUT AU CHAMPAGNE

Another recipe combining tropical coral trout with champagne! This one's a specialty of Verandah's Restaurant.

Poach *4 coral trout fillets* in *1 bottle champagne* and a squeeze of *¼ lemon*. When cooked, remove fish and keep warm.

Pour poaching liquid from pan and reserve. To the pan add:
2 tablespoons butter
60 g (2 oz) blanched almonds
½ cup white grapes
squeeze of lemon
When almonds have turned golden, add:
½ cup reserved juice
30 ml (1 oz) cream
parsley
salt and pepper
Stir until sauce simmers.

Arrange fish on plate, pour sauce over. Add parsley and serve with *steamed potatoes* and a *green salad*.
Serves 4.

TROUT WITH CRAB

Clean and scale *2 trout*. Brush with *1 tablespoon lemon juice* and *30 g (1 oz) melted butter*. Sprinkle with *salt and pepper*.
Stuff each trout with *stuffing*.
Combine together:
½ cup fresh breadcrumbs
1 teaspoon French mustard
1 small onion, chopped
200 g (6 oz) fresh or canned crab
1 tablespoon mayonnaise
¼ cup chopped parsley
Place trout into a greased baking dish, and bake in a hot oven 200°C (400°F) for 10–12 minutes or until flesh of fish flakes.
Serve with *lemon sauce*.
In a food processor or electric blender, lightly combine:
3 egg yolks
2 tablespoons lemon juice
¼ teaspoon dry mustard
Pour in *125 g (4 oz) melted butter* in a steady stream, beating all the time.
Whip *½ cup cream* until soft peaks form, add *1 teaspoon lemon juice* and mix well. Gently fold the butter mixture into the cream and serve with the trout.
Serves 2.

PAN FRIED CORAL TROUT

Slice trout into fillets and sprinkle with *a little salt and lemon juice*.
Heat some *butter* in a pan and fry fish approximately 3 minutes each side.
Serve with *fresh salad* and *whole baked potatoes*.

BARNACLE BILL'S

Vic Piccone's father, Vittorio, migrated from Italy and arrived in Cairns about 1935 to work in the canefields. He married a local girl, Edith Alice Remilton, whose father worked on the Kuranda Railway. Remilton was very community minded, active in the local show association, and the G. A. Remilton stand at Cairns Showground was dedicated to his memory.

Vittorio opened a butcher shop which he operated until just before the end of World War II; then he went into the construction business for a while. Eventually returning to the butchery business, he also opened a restaurant called 'Tropicana' in 1962.

After his death in 1969 the Piccone family continued to operate the Tropicana until they sold it about 1974. The restaurant was renamed 'Barnacle Bill's' and is still a very popular seafood restaurant on the Esplanade.

Vic Piccone recalls the restaurant's early days when there was only one other major restaurant in town — the Kowloon, a Chinese restaurant in Lake Street. The Tropicana specialised in seafood, especially barramundi and coral trout for which people used to queue up outside, and quite often pandemonium prevailed! Sometimes if the restaurant ran out of these delicacies, or found them unavailable, the customers nearly went beserk!

Vic Piccone is one of three children born to Vittoria and Edith. The Piccone family enjoys the Cairns lifestyle and Vic is firmly entrenched as a contributing citizen to the local community.

BARNACLE BILL'S MORETON BAY BUGS IN BEER BATTER

A simple and simply delicious dish.

Dust shelled *green bugs* with *flour*, dip in *beer batter* (see recipe on page 27) and deep fry — about 5 minutes.

Serve on a bed of *rice* with *chilli plum sauce*.

Note: Home-made plum sauce may be used, with chilli powder *or* chilli sauce added to taste. It depends how hot you like it!

BARNACLE BILL'S BEAUTY

Chef Tim Norris says this is a very popular dish, comprising hot and cold seafood attractively presented.

A precooked combination of *Moreton Bay bugs, jewelfish* (a reef fish), *prawns* and *calamari* is mixed with a *seafood sauce* and arranged on a bed of *shredded lettuce* in an iced bowl-shaped champagne glass.

Seafood sauce

For 4 servings you'll need:

1 *cup mayonnaise*
½ *cup tomato sauce*
1 *tablespoon worcestershire sauce*
a nip of brandy, or to taste

On the same platter, in a suitably sized clam shell, arrange a hot collection of the same seafoods.

All except the calamari are dusted with flour, dipped in *beer batter*, deep fried for a few minutes, then drained and served. The calamari rings are crumbed and deep fried.

Beer batter

To make enough for 4 servings, beat lightly 2 *eggs*. With a fork fold in:

⅓ *cup plain flour*
pinch salt

Stir in ⅓ *cup milk* and beat with the fork in a rapid folding motion (it aerates the mixture).

Just before cooking, beat in ⅓ *cup beer*.

To serve, any remaining space on the platter is filled with small slices of luscious fresh Queensland fruits — *pawpaw, watermelon, pineapple, rockmelon* — plus *passionfruit, tomato, capsicum and alfalfa*.

A feast and a half!

Serves 4.

NAUTILUS RESTAURANT, PORT DOUGLAS

One of Queensland's best loved restaurants, the Nautilus, had its humble beginnings in 1964 when Port Douglas residents, Diana and Max Bowden, opened for business. With so many people coming to the area and nowhere to eat, Diana saw the need for such an establishment. Her cooking facilities were very basic — an old primus stove did most of the work!

Sunday became the restaurant's special day, and visitors enjoyed the tropical outdoors and the Bowdens' own special brand of hospitality. The Nautilus did not cater for evening meals in its early days because the roads were too hazardous for travellers, particularly between Cairns and Port Douglas — people were not game to make the trip at night!

In the early 1980s the Nautilus was bought by Diane Cilento and her husband, Tony Schaeffer.

In 1985 the now famous restaurant was acquired by an equally famous chef, Mogens Bay Esbensen, who owns Butlers restaurant at Potts Point in Sydney. While retaining Butlers, Mogens now resides at Port Douglas and hopes to operate a cooking school, as he has done so successfully in his Sydney restaurant.

He is very familiar with tropical produce, having spent many years in Thailand, and regards the acquisition of the Nautilus as a new challenge and extension of his talents. Cooking is his life. Starting as an apprentice chef in his native Denmark, Mogens has worked in many parts of the world.

Set in lush tropical gardens, the restaurant has been given a facelift with the installation of a new kitchen and lovely antique furniture. In a superb position overlooking Port Douglas, the Nautilus, already renowned for its exotic cuisine, looks set to continue its attraction for visitors from all over the world.

Port Douglas, founded in 1877 as a port to serve the Hodgkinson goldfields, has, since 1956, functioned mainly as a fishing and tourist centre. It is from this port that many fishing boats leave for the Great Barrier Reef. Many visitors come too, just to enjoy the pretty tropical village and its beautiful beach and later return to settle for the solitude and beauty it offers. Nautilus restaurant's new occupant is one of those.

MARINATED GOLDEN TREVALLY

Any firm-fleshed fish can be used for this dish — the Nautilus chef uses golden trevally because of its ready availability in Port Douglas.

Fillet *1 kg (2 lb) fish*, cut the fillet off the skin and cut away the boned section. Clean the fillets well.

Heat *a little olive oil* in a frying pan and seal the fish for about two minutes on each side.

Transfer to a glass or stainless steel dish.

Remove the *zest from 5 limes and 3 oranges* and blanch the zest.

Squeeze the juice from the fruit and, after salting the fish with *sea salt*, pour the juices over.

Sprinkle the blanched zest over the fish with the julienne (thin strips) of *6 red chillies*. (It's advisable to wear gloves to handle chillies — they can burn.)

Marinate 12 hours or overnight in the refrigerator, turning the fish twice.

Serve with thin julienne of peeled *white radish* crisped in iced water, and leaves of *fresh basil, dill or mint*.

Serves 4.

FISH IN CORNMEAL CRUST WITH AVOCADO

Toss *4 fish steaks* in *½ cup wholemeal flour* seasoned with *salt and pepper*. Dip in mixture of *1 egg* and *1 tablespoon milk*, then in *½ cup yellow cornmeal (palenta)*. Shallow fry in hot *oil* until tender. Serve with *dressing*.

Peel *1 small avocado* and seed *1 cucumber*. Combine both in a processor or blender with:

1 tablespoon chopped shallots
2 small cloves garlic, crushed
2 tablespoons lemon juice
¼ cup cream

Season with *salt and pepper*.

Serves 4.

MOUSSE OF SCALLOPS AND SAFFRON WITH CORAL SAUCE

Remove the orange roe from *12 plump scallops* and set aside.

Process until smooth:

¼ *teaspoon powdered saffron*
roughly chopped scallops
6 tablespoons creme fraiche (see below)
3 egg yolks
1 egg white
500 ml (1 pint) fish stock

Butter six ramekin dishes and fill to within 5 mm (¼ in) of the top with the scallop mixture.

Bake in the oven in a bath of water for 10 minutes on moderate heat 180°C (350°F).

For the *sauce*, saute the scallop roe in *25 g (1 oz) butter* for a minute. Place in a blender with *4 tablespoons creme fraiche* and *500 ml (1 pint) fish stock*. Process until smooth. Strain into a heavy pan and gently heat, without boiling, adding *salt and pepper* to taste.

Unmould the mousses onto heated plates, pour the sauce around the mousse with just a little over the top. Garnish with fresh *tarragon or chervil*.

Serves 6.

Creme fraiche

In a saucepan mix:

600 ml (1 pint) cream
300 ml (½ pint) buttermilk, sour cream or yoghurt

Heat gently just until the mixture is no longer cold. Pour into a container and partially cover. Leave at room temperature till thick and slightly acid, about 6–8 hrs, depending on the temperature. Stir, cover and refrigerate.

TAWNY'S RESTAURANT

This waterfront restaurant, one of Cairns' most popular, serves some of the best seafood I've tasted. On my last visit I had the freshest, most delicious barramundi, grilled and slathered with sauteed almonds (the recipe for this dish appears below). Friends had mud crab, which took about thirty minutes of enjoyable eating, and grilled lobster, all freshly caught.

In a delightful setting adjacent to the Game Fishing Club, the waterfront view is always interesting.

BARRAMUNDI ALMONDINE

Season enough *barramundi fillets* for four people, coat with *flour*. Dot with *butter* and grill until cooked on both sides, then cover one side of each fillet with *slivered almonds*. Grill until almonds just turn brown.

To serve, remove from pan to plates, squeeze *lemon juice* into the butter remaining in the grill pan, and pour over top of fillets.

Serves 4.

PRAWNS AND PINENUTS IN TOMATO SAUCE

Fry until transparent in 1 *tablespoon butter*:
1 *clove crushed garlic*
1 *large onion*, chopped finely
Add 4 *ripe chopped tomatoes* and cook until tender.

Add and stir in:
1 *tablespoon tomato paste*, diluted in ½ *cup water*
½ *cup red wine*
1 *kg (2 lb) shelled green prawns*
Add and simmer until prawns are just tender and sauce has thickened:
½ *cup cream*
pinch nutmeg
pinch freshly chopped or dried basil
handful of pinenuts
250 *g (8 oz) crumbled fetta cheese*
Sprinkle with chopped *parsley* and serve on a *bed of boiled noodles or rice.*

Serves 6.

On Barramundi

The future of the barramundi, bred to pan size and served whole, could lie in a tin shed on a narrow wharf in the Northern Queensland town of Cairns. There, marine biologists Dr. Mick Heasman and Jim Ryall of 'Sea Hatcheries' are hatching and raising fish for what they say is a promising eating and angling industry, as well as an industry for aboriginal and islander communities.

They plan, depending on funding, a multi-species hatching of barramundi, marine prawns and mud crabs.

Northern Daily Leader
14 March 1985

BAKED SCHNAPPER

Combine in a bowl and mix well:
1½ cups cooked rice
1 stick celery, diced
½ cup chopped green pepper
1 onion, peeled and chopped
salt and pepper
Stuff *a whole washed and scaled schnapper, about 2 kg (4 lb)*, and place in a well-greased baking dish.

Melt *90 g (3 oz) butter* in a pan, remove from heat and add:
3 tablespoons lemon juice
1 tablespoon grated ginger
1 teaspoon soy sauce
6 chopped shallots
salt and pepper
Pour over fish and bake uncovered in a moderately slow oven 150°C (300°F) for 40–50 minutes or until fish is cooked, basting frequently with juices while cooking.

Halfway through cooking, place layers of *1 sliced onion* and *1 sliced tomato* over fish.

When cooked, place fish in a serving dish, pour pan juices over and sprinkle with *2 tablespoons finely chopped parsley*.

Serves 4–6.

FATHOMS RESTAURANT

Fathoms, a delightful timber residence set among lush tropical trees and flowers, has operated as a restaurant since the late 1970s.

Original owners of the house were the Kennedy family who lived there for about twenty years before selling it to the National Bank. The house was used as a bank residence for some years and was in turn sold to Don McMillan of McMillan Real Estate.

In 1976 Fathoms restaurant began on another site. Its rapid expansion made a move necessary and this present site was converted to Fathoms restaurant a couple of years later. Well known as one of Queensland's best, the restaurant was acquired by Tony Roach and Chris Berry in 1982.

They made extensive alterations to the building — relocating the bar so that patrons could relax in comfort, altering the reception area, enclosing the verandah and installing air conditioning. While some might query the necessity of the latter, the reason is clear to those who dined on the open verandah a few years ago. Nasties abound in the tropical night air — mosquitoes, 'midgies' and other flying insects. Additionally, smoke from the regular cane fires caused some discomfort and many sooty tablecloths!

With the emphasis on seafoods, soon after Chris and Tony took over they created 'Barramundi Fathoms', and the dish became synonymous with Fathoms. Indeed, another north Queensland restaurant includes on its menu 'Coral Trout Fathoms'. A compliment to the chef!

Fathoms changed hands in 1985, the new owners maintaining the standard of this excellent restaurant.

BARRAMUNDI FATHOMS

Fathoms is one of northern Queensland's best known restaurants and is famous for this dish.

For each serving use *a slice of barramundi, about 185 g (6 oz)*, and for the filling use a combination of chopped *fresh prawns, bugs, fish and scallops, seasoned* and combined with a *knob of butter.*

Place the required quantity on the fish slice and roll up.

Wrap in *buttered filo pastry*, seal ends and bake on a tray in a moderate oven 180°C (350°F) until browned and cooked. It may be crisped under the griller before serving.

Top with *hollandaise sauce.*

FATHOMS BON FEMME

This delicious dish is a specialty when fresh Tasmanian scallops are available.

First make a *cream sauce* (white butter sauce made with fish stock).

For *250 g (8 oz) fresh scallops*, you'll need about *500 ml (1 ¾ cups)* sauce.

To the sauce add:
½ cup dry white wine
1 teaspoon chopped fresh herbs
6 medium mushrooms, peeled and sliced
2 rashers bacon, de-rinded and chopped

Add the scallops and simmer the lot gently until the sauce is reduced to a smooth consistency. Do not overcook or scallops will be tough.

Serve topped with just a little *hollandaise sauce.*
Serves 4.

CURRIED PRAWNS WITH MANGO

Shell and devein *500 g (1 lb) green prawns*, rinse under cold water and pat dry. Add to a mixture of *2 teaspoons cornflour, 1 teaspoon salt* and *1 egg white*, and mix well. Allow to stand for 1 hour.

Heat *1 cup oil* in a frypan, add prawns and fry quickly for 2 minutes or until just cooked. Remove from pan and drain well on absorbent paper. Drain off oil from pan, leaving approximately 2 tablespoons, and saute *1 large chopped onion* for 2 minutes. Add:
1 teaspoon curry powder
2 teaspoons bottled sate sauce
¼ cup canned coconut milk

Bring to boil and simmer for one minute, stirring constantly. Add:
2 ripe mangoes, peeled and sliced
½ red capsicum, thinly sliced
2 chopped shallots
the prawns

Combine well and heat through. Season with *salt and pepper* and serve sprinkled with *extra chopped shallots.*
Serves 4.

THE FRANKLIN
NORTH QUEENSLAND ENGINEERING AGENTS (NQEA)

Undoubtedly the world's best equipped oceanographic research vessel, the R.V. *Franklin* was completed in 1985. Building began at NQEA in 1983 and the naming ceremony was conducted by Her Excellency Lady Stephen, wife of Australia's Governor-General, at the end of 1984.

With a crew of thirteen and twelve scientists, the *Franklin* left Cairns in April 1985 bound for her home base, Australia's major oceanographic establishment, the CSIRO Division of Oceanography in Hobart, Tasmania. The ship represents Australia's major means of physical, chemical and biological research in open waters of our region.

The man responsible for NQEA's establishment is Mr Richard George Fry, CBE, founder and present chairman of the company. Born in Cairns, his father came to the town as a railway worker and was one of those stalwart men responsible for the Cairns–Kuranda line.

After serving in the AIF as an electrician, Richard Fry returned to Cairns and in 1948 began his own engineering business in partnership with Don Ryan — buying him out five years later. They operated from the Fry residence with a staff of three and two hundred pounds in army pay.

Fry's first client was the local sawmill and from that small beginning, the business has developed into a fully integrated self-supporting engineering activity in Australia's north. The workforce peaked at 850 during the 1983/84 patrol boat construction contract for the Royal Australian Navy. A justifiable reward was the Australian Defence Industry Quality and Achievement Award for 1983.

NQEA's expertise in shipbuilding and ship repairs (both commercial and military), mining and sugar milling equipment has led to successful sales in Australia and overseas.

One of two sons, Don Fry took over the company as managing director in 1978 and for him the most satisfying aspect of the job is the constant challenge. Of all the company's achievements, the pinnacle for Don was the navy patrol boat construction. NQEA produced four patrol boats per year for four years.

The years have seen NQEA's unparalleled contribution to the north's development as a major shipbuilding and maritime industries servicing centre.

TUNA RISSOLES

Combine in a bowl and mix together thoroughly:
4 slices crustless wholemeal bread, cubed
1 large onion, sliced
1 large tomato, sliced
1 small capsicum, sliced
2 x 450 g (16 oz) tins tuna in brine, drained (reserve liquid)
Add:
1 tablespoon tomato paste
salt and pepper
2 tablespoons lemon juice
Make a roux with:
2 heaped tablespoons flour
2 tablespoons butter
half the reserved tuna liquid
Add to the tuna mixture, make patties, and refrigerate for half an hour. Roll in seasoned flour and return to fridge.

Heat oil in a pan, roll rissoles in some flour a second time, and fry until golden brown on both sides.

Serve with salad and crispy potato chips.

Serves 8 as a main course.

Note: These are equally good hot or cold and are particularly good as small balls for a starter.

For a slight variation as a starter, instead of a second rolling in flour, roll in almond flakes before shallow frying.

PACIFIC CHILLI BUGS AND PRAWNS

Peel 500 g (1 lb) green prawns and 500 g (1 lb) Moreton Bay bugs and marinate for about one hour in a mixture of 2 level teaspoons of cornflour and ½ cup of cold water (this is a tenderising method often used in Chinese cooking).

Drain the seafood and stir-fry in hot oil just covering the base of a heavy pan. Remove to another dish.

In the same pan stir-fry 200 g (6 oz) shallots and 50 g (1½ oz) minced fresh ginger with a little more oil.

Then add:
the seafood
juice of one large lemon
2 teaspoons sambal oelek (available in Asian food stores)
2 teaspoons oyster sauce — or more if desired
If a thicker mixture is desired stir in another *2 level teaspoons cornflour* mixed with *½ cup of cold water.*
Serves 4.

CRAB CREPES

Make eight of your favourite savoury crepes, then proceed as follows.

Melt *2 tablespoons butter* in a pan and add:
2 cups crab meat (fresh cooked or canned)
125 g (4 oz) sliced mushrooms
¼ teaspoon thyme
1 tablespoon chopped parsley
1 clove garlic, crushed
3 tablespoons flour

Cook for 30 seconds, then pour over *3 tablespoons white wine* and *4 tablespoons rich chicken stock* and cook until the mushrooms and crab meat are in a thick sauce — add more stock if necessary.

Stir in *4 tablespoons cream*, and remove from heat.

Fill each crepe with the mixture and fold in quarters or roll up. Place into buttered casserole dish, mask with the following *bechamel sauce*, and sprinkle with a mixture of *1 tablespoon parmesan cheese* and *2 tablespoons breadcrumbs.*

Bake in a 180°C (350°F) oven until heated through and top is brown.

Bechamel sauce
Melt *2 tablespoons butter*, add *2 tablespoons flour* and stir until combined, cook for 2–3 minutes. Do not brown roux. Gradually add *1½–2 cups milk*, stirring constantly to prevent lumps, simmer 2–3 minutes. Season to taste.
Serves 8.

PRAWN SOUFFLE QUICHE

Pastry

In the bowl of an electric food processor process *2 cups plain flour* and *125 g (4 oz) butter* until mixture resembles fine breadcrumbs. While processor is operating add *a squeeze of lemon juice* and enough *water* to form a smooth dough. Allow pastry to rest for about twenty minutes.

Roll out thinly and line a well-greased 20 cm (8 in) springform pan. Sprinkle with *½ cup grated cheese* and *125 g (4 oz) green prawns*.

Refrigerate while you make the *filling*.

In a saucepan melt *3 tablespoons butter* and saute *6 chopped shallots* and *6 button mushrooms* for 1–2 minutes. Stir in *4 tablespoons flour*.

Add:

1 cup milk
½ cup cream

Stir until mixture boils and thickens.

Mix in:

1 teaspoon prepared mustard
salt and pepper
6 egg yolks   } combined
1 tablespoon lemon juice
1 teaspoon finely grated lemon rind

Remove from heat.

Whip *6 egg whites* until soft peaks form then gently fold into sauce. Pour into pastry case and sprinkle with *½ cup grated cheese* and *125 g (4 oz) green prawns*.

Bake in a 220°C (450°F) oven for 20 minutes, then reduce temperature to 180°C (350°F) and cook a further 25–30 minutes. Serve immediately.

Serves 6.

* M·E·A·T & P·O·U·L·T·R·Y *

Here are some of the most delicious dishes imaginable — many utilising the exotic fruits of the tropics.

PORK FILLET AND AVOCADO APHRODITE

This was champion recipe in the 1984 National Avocado Chef Championship Awards.

Trim *2 medium-sized pork fillets* and cut each in half. Flatten carefully between plastic.

Finely chop *2 onions* and cook, covered, for 4–5 minutes. Cool, then add *150 g (5 oz) grated mozzarella cheese* and mix well.

Blanch *8 small button mushrooms* in either *stock or water* with a *squeeze of lemon juice* for about 30 seconds.

Place some of the cheese mixture in the centre of the flattened pork fillet, add 2 mushrooms and a generous slice of *avocado*. Add more cheese and another slice of avocado.

Roll up the fillet carefully to enclose the filling. Coat each fillet in *plain flour (about ½ cup)* then dip into *2 beaten eggs*. Coat with *200 g (6 oz) macadamia nuts*, finely chopped, pressing on firmly. Shallow fry carefully in *heated clarified butter or a little oil* until golden. Finish in a moderately hot oven 200°C(400°F) for 5-10 minutes.

Serve with *sauce*.

Heat *150 g (5 oz) butter* until it starts to colour — not brown. Add the *juice of 1 lemon* and *2 to 3 sprigs of fresh tarragon*. Pour over the fillets and serve immediately.

Serves 4.

ABBOTT MANOR

Sadly no longer standing, this building was destroyed by fire early in 1986.

Because Abbott Manor was such a landmark reflecting an important stage in the history of Cairns its story is related here. The accompanying sketch is undoubtedly one of the last completed before the building's destruction.

The home was built in 1908 for Mr Adam John Pettigrew McDonnell by the architect Harvey Draper who designed many Cairns buildings including the *Cairns Post* building also in Abbott Street. Mr McDonnell was a founder of the firm of solicitors, McDonnell, Harris and Co., in existence for over a hundred years.

Large grounds surrounded the house, extending to Lake Street, and included croquet lawns and stables. Gracious living was the order of the day and no doubt reflected the hard work and resultant success of the pioneers.

A prominent name in the Cairns history books, Mr A. J. Draper was, in 1918, the next owner of Abbott Manor. Affectionately dubbed 'The Father of Cairns', he was seven times elected as mayor, was a prominent businessman and staunch promoter of the development of Cairns. In 1901 Draper became owner of the *Cairns Post*, which remained in the control of his family until 1965.

The delightful house was purchased by Burns Philp in 1937 for use by their managers. Still a notable business concern, Burns Philp was the trading company responsible for opening up trade in the Pacific region.

One manager and his wife, Mr and Mrs William Dupane, formerly of Port Moresby, lived in Abbott Manor for twenty-two years. They became very much a part of Cairns society and entertained lavishly over the years. Another Burns Philp manager, Mr Rex Noble, lived there from 1960 until his death in 1963. Subsequent owners of the house were Dr Russell Wilson, Mr Curtain from New Guinea and Dr W. McGovern of Cairns.

Ghost stories relating to the house were laid to rest when, according to reports, a Bishop of the Church of England conducted a ceremony to exorcise the unwanted 'resident' spirit!

Abbott Manor was turned into a reception centre in 1977, and during the process of alterations the remarkable craftsmanship of its builder became evident. Most of the timber used was red cedar

and all measurements were found to be exact, from the breezeways above the French doors to the dining room, to the panes of glass in each door.

BRAISED PORK CHOPS AND PRUNES WITH DILL AND PAPRIKA SAUCE

Mix together:
1 tablespoon sweet paprika
flour for coating 4 chump pork chops
salt and pepper
Coat chops and fry in a *small quantity of heated lard* for about 4 minutes each side. Transfer to a dish.

Add to a pan and saute until shallots are transparent:
12 pitted prunes
2 shallots, chopped
½ teaspoon chopped garlic
Off the heat, add 2 *tablespoons redcurrant jelly*, and stir.

Return the chops to the pan and pour in *300 ml (½ pint) chicken stock*. Simmer until stock is reduced by half. Remove pork chops and keep warm.

Beat 4 *tablespoons each thickened cream and sour cream* in a bowl and blend in *1 tablespoon flour*. Pour into pan and stir, simmering for 2–3 minutes. Add 3 *tablespoons finely chopped dill* and the chops and simmer slowly for 5–10 minutes. Serve immediately. *Serves 4.*

BAKED HAM

Soak *raw ham* overnight in cold water.

Make a dough of *plain flour* and *water* — a thick dough, not too wet. Pat out on a bench, and sprinkle all over with *ground cloves*.
Place ham in middle of dough, cover all over so it is well sealed. Wrap in a *clean cotton cloth*, to keep dough together.

Bake at 190°C (390°F) on the third shelf, by weight of ham:
½ hour for first 500 g (1 lb)
¼ hour each additional 500 g (1 lb)
Leave in baked dough covering in baking dish until the next day.
Break open, remove skin and cover with dry cooked *breadcrumbs* to which have been added *a small amount of crushed olives*.

PORK CHOPS IN WINE

Brown *10 to 12 large loin pork chops*, trimmed of excess fat, in *1 tablespoon heated oil*. Remove and place in two baking dishes. Drain the pan of any excess fat.

Cut into bite-sized pieces and saute lightly in the same pan (about 3 minutes):
1 *large capsicum*
2 *large onions*
3 *sticks celery*

Whisk together the following ingredients, then add to vegetables:
1 *cup water*
1 x 440 *(15 oz) g tin tomato puree (or soup)*
1 x 440 *(15 oz) g tin cream of chicken soup*
1 *cup white wine*

Bring to the boil, remove from heat and pour over chops.

Bake in a moderate oven 180°C (350°F) for approximately 1 hour or until chops are tender.

Serve with *boiled rice* to which *a little butter* and some *toasted almonds or salted cashews* have been added.

Serves 8–10.

Note: This is equally good with chicken instead of pork chops — Use 2 chickens cut into serving-sized pieces.

VEAL MACADAMIA WITH PLANTAIN

Flatten *6 slices veal* with a mallet, as for schnitzels. Spread over one side of the steaks:
1 *plantain or 2 cavendish bananas*, sliced
salt and pepper
6 *tablespoons crushed macadamia nuts*, toasted

Fold slices over and secure with toothpicks. Dust veal with *flour* (¼ *cup*) then dip carefully in 2 *beaten eggs* and coat with *breadcrumbs*. Place in refrigerator for at least 1 hour before cooking.

Heat *oil* to cover bottom of a pan and cook veal for 5 minutes on each side on gentle heat.

Serve garnished with *choppped parsley and lemon wedges*.

Serves 6.

BARBECUED SPARERIBS

Heat 2 *tablespoons oil* in a large frying pan over moderate heat. When the oil is hot, add *1 clove crushed garlic* and *1 large, finely chopped onion* and cook for 3 minutes, stirring frequently until the onion is translucent and soft but not brown.

Add and stir well:
4 *tablespoons worcestershire sauce*
1 *cup tomato puree*
3 *tablespoons lemon juice*
½ *teaspoon salt*
¼ *teaspoon black pepper*
½ *teaspoon dried sage*
4 *tablespoons light brown sugar*
2 *teaspoons mustard*
½ *cup beef stock*

Simmer over a low heat 5-10 minutes, stirring frequently. Remove from heat.

Marinate *1½ kg (3 lb) beef spareribs* in this mixture for a few hours, then place ribs on a rack and cook in a hot oven 200°C (400°F) for 1 hour or until brown and crisp, basting with the barbecue sauce every 15 minutes.

Serves 6–8.

BEEF WITH SAVOURY BUTTER

Sear a *2-3 kg (4–6 lb) fillet of beef* in *hot oil*. Slice almost through, but leave the slices attached at the base, rather like preparing garlic bread. You will probably get 6–8 slices.

Place *2 chopped shallots* into a small saucepan and add *2 tablespoons white wine*. Boil till the wine has practically evaporated.

Cream 125 g (4 oz) butter with *2 cloves crushed garlic* and *2 tablespoons parsley* and add the shallots and wine.

Add 4 *tablespoons breadcrumbs* and 4 *tablespoons grated cheese*.

Spread the savoury butter between each beef slice and across the top and sides.

Tie neatly and securely with string. Bake in a preheated moderate oven 180°C (350°F) for around 20 minutes for rare beef, more if you like it well done.

Serves 6–8.

TROPICAL FRUIT CURRY

Sear *1½ kg (3 lb) diced beef* in a large pan in *2 tablespoons heated oil*. Add *1 tablespoon curry powder* and cook for 2 minutes.

Add and continue to cook:
1 carrot, diced
1 onion, finely chopped
1 apple, diced
1 potato, diced

Add *1 tablespoon flour*, cook for a couple of minutes, then add:
1 tablespoon sultanas
1 dessertspoon plum jam
1 tablespoon fruit chutney
seasoning to taste
1½–2 cups brown stock

Simmer till meat is tender, about 1½ hours, stirring occasionally to ensure sauce does not burn on base of pot.
Serves 6–8.

PARADISE CASSEROLE

Toss *1 kg (2 lb) cubed chuck steak* in *2 tablespoons plain flour* and *½ teaspoon ground ginger*, then brown in *2 tablespoons oil*. Remove from pan.

In the same oil, *saute 2 sticks diced celery* and *3 sliced onions* for a few minutes. Replace steak and add:
1 cup beef stock
½ cup vinegar
1 can tomatoes, drained
½ cup brown sugar
salt and pepper

Cover and cook until tender, about 2 hours.

During the last 30 minutes, add:
3 medium carrots, sliced
1 x 440 g (15 oz) can crushed pineapple, drained
½ cup raisins soaked in ½ cup pineapple juice.
Serves 6.

CAIRNS WAR MEMORIAL

The war memorial in Cairns originally took the form of a memorial clock, the foundation stone of which was laid by A. J. Draper in 1925. It was unveiled on 25 April (Anzac Day) 1926.

The memorial stood guard at the intersection of Abbott and Shields streets until 1972, when it was considered a traffic hazard and moved to its present peaceful site on the Esplanade. Now minus the clock, the memorial's main feature is the statue of the unknown soldier gazing out to sea from the surrounding coconut palms. It stands for those who have given their lives in all wars.

Directly opposite, on the Esplanade, is the RSL headquarters — a development of the original organisation formed after World War I, 'to provide for the sick and wounded and needy among those who served, and their dependents'. The league also provides social activities for members and wives. The Cairns sub-branch enrolled its first members in 1916 and acquired its first rest home in 1919.

While Cairns' contribution to World War I was a significant one, World War II was much closer to home, especially after the fall of Singapore.

After the bombing of Darwin by 180 Japanese planes in February 1942, the gravity of the war situation was keenly felt in Cairns and the government closed all schools in the far north and Queensland's coastal belt. The population of Cairns was about halved. Some residents just walked out of their homes; other houses were up for sale for a song. Cairns, Australia's northernmost established port after Darwin, became the country's most important.

The Coral Sea Battle, which began in May 1942, brought the war frighteningly close to the north Queensland coast. In the same month Townsville was bombed, and in July a single Japanese plane dropped a bomb, unexploded, on a farmhouse at Mossman. The year 1942 saw the arrival of American troops in the Cairns region and some two million were dependent on the city's resources. They built roads, airfields, sheds, wharves and igloos, took over the Strand Hotel for the Red Cross and used the Pacific Hotel for a club.

The Battle of the Coral Sea, fought with bombers from Townsville, Mareeba and other northern airports, marked the turning point for the war as it related to north Queensland. It was

a terrifying time for Australia, with imposed blackouts and food rationing emphasising the ever-present threat of invasion. Thanks to Australian and United States defence personnel, we live to tell the tale.

Catalina flying boats also played an important role in World War II. Cairns was their operational base, and in the city centennial year, a memorial to the Catalina crews was unveiled on the Esplanade, overlooking the waters from which they took off. A bronze plaque bears a detailed inscription, part of which reads:

'It was perhaps unique among the settled communitites of Australia in having a fraction of its population in almost daily contact with her enemies, and in pulsing night and day to the passage of armed aircraft directly attacking them.

In those far off years this placid spot resounded some 3000 times to the labouring take off of a loaded Catalina, and a day later heard its whispering return — but not 3000 times. From all Australian Catalina operations in the Southwest Pacific theatre three hundred and twenty airmen failed to return.'

A happy sequel for one Catalina, A24-35, was its purchase in 1947 by Captain Stewart Middlemiss who served with Squadrons 11 and 43. With a partner he formed Barrier Reef Airways and the old war plane's last days were spent transporting passengers to the islands of the Barrier Reef.

Wartime Advertisement

Our fighting men need all the Vegemite we can possibly let them have. They need it because it plays such a vital part in guarding them against that insidious 'fifth columnist' — dietary deficiency.

In sharing available supplies of Vegemite with our fighting forces you and your family are definitely helping the war effort. So if your local shop has less Vegemite these days, there's a sound reason why, the boys behind the guns need all the Vegemite we can give them.

Cairns Post
1942

PINEAPPLE LAMB STEW

Heat 1 tablespoon *each butter and oil* in a heavy pan and brown 1 kg (2 lb) *cubed boneless lamb*, adding a single layer to the pan at a time. Remove to a plate.

Reduce heat and add 1 *chopped onion*. Cook gently until soft.
Add:
juice from 1 x 440 g (15 oz) can pineapple pieces
¼ cup dry white wine
1 tablespoon soy sauce
1 tablespoon tomato sauce
½ teaspoon ground ginger

Return the lamb to the pan and add *salt and pepper* to taste. Cover and simmer for ½ to 1 hour or until lamb is tender. Add the pineapple pieces and cook 5 minutes more.

Mix 1 tablespoon *flour* with a little *cold water* and thicken the stew, then boil gently for 2 minutes.

Heat 1 tablespoon *butter* in a frying pan and toss for 2–3 minutes:
½ cup sliced celery
½–1 cup pecan nuts

The celery should remain crisp.

Turn stew into a serving dish and sprinkle with celery and pecans.

Serve with *boiled rice or noodles*.

Serves 6.

APRICOT BEEF

Dice 1 kg (2 lb) *blade steak* and brown, in a pan or cast iron casserole, in 2 *tablespoons heated oil*.

Mix together and add to steak in pan:
1 x 425 ml (¾ pint) can apricot nectar
1 pkt french onion soup
1 x 440 g (15 oz) can crushed pineapple
½ teaspoon powdered ginger

Place lid on pan and simmer for 2 hours. Thicken if necessary.

Garnish with *chopped parsley* and *croutons*.

Serves 4–6.

SWEET AND SOUR PORK

Cut *500 g (1 lb) pork fillet* into cubes, coat in *⅓ cup cornflour*, stir fry in a little oil in an electric skillet until golden brown and cooked.

Drain and keep warm while you make the *sauce:*

Blend *⅓ cup cornflour* in a saucepan with *1½ cups chicken stock*. Bring to the boil and add:

½ cup vinegar
⅔ cup brown sugar
1 teaspoon salt
2 tablespoons soy sauce
1 clove garlic, crushed
1 green capsicum, chopped
1 or 2 sticks celery, finely chopped
1 large onion, sliced
500 g (1 lb) pineapple pieces
3 tablespoons grated orange rind
¼ cup orange juice
¼ cup pineapple juice
2 carrots, sliced and blanched

Simmer for 10 minutes, then add:

¼ cup shallots, sliced
½ a cucumber, sliced and quartered

Cook for a further minute, then serve with *rice*.

Serves 4.

BOILED TURKEY

Mix *2 eggs* into the *juice of one lemon*. Fry *250 g (8 oz) onions*, finely chopped, and the same amount of *celery*, in *125 g (4 oz) heated butter*. Don't brown.

Mix together in a bowl:

2 loaves stale bread, made into breadcrumbs
4 tablespoons chopped parsley
rind of 1 lemon

Add the onions and celery, eggs, and some *salt and pepper*.

Stuff a *3 kg (6 lb) turkey*. Use pins on neck after stuffing that end. Stuff rest at rear end. When completed, cover with foil and sew up, so it won't split.

Bend wings back, tie around parson's nose, then around 1 leg at a time, then back around wing to hold together.

Stock

In a large heavy saucepan, place turkey breast side up and just cover with water.

Add:

1 turnip
1 outside stick of celery
3 whole onions, with 3 cloves stuck in each
12 peppercorns
1 heaped tablespoon salt
2 bayleaves
3 unpeeled, sliced carrots
some parsley sprigs and stalks

Bring to boil and simmer for 1½ to 2 hours.

Turkey sauce

Melt 125 g (4 oz) butter and stew 1 large bunch celery, chopped, with some salt and pepper. Cover and simmer for about 20–30 minutes. It must not brown.

When cooked, mix with bechamel sauce.

Melt 90 g (3 oz) butter, add 90 g (3 oz) flour and 600 ml (1 pint) boiled milk and stir. Add salt and pepper to taste and when thick, cover with lid.

After adding turkey sauce, simmer for 5 minutes then place in blender for a few seconds. Return to saucepan and stir in 300 ml (½ pint) cream.

To serve turkey:

Place turkey on a large dish and when slightly cooled, cover with sauce. Garnish with parsley.

Serves 8.

Note: The turkey must be fresh and young.

SEASONING BALLS

Make a seasoning as if for stuffing chicken:

3 cups white soft breadcrumbs
1 teaspoon herbs
1 onion, chopped, and sauteed in 1 dessertspoon butter
fresh chopped mint
1 raw egg

Form into balls and roll in flour. Cook in a baking dish with chicken, lamb, etc.

MULGRAVE SHIRE COUNCIL OFFICES

Situated on the Esplanade overlooking the Pacific Ocean, this attractive building was constructed in 1912 by successful tenderers, Wilson and Bailey.

The original building was sited in the middle of the block and featured open verandahs clearly visible from most aspects and approaches. Materials used were timber for the floors and internal partitions, tendered brick and/or concrete for the walls and cement plaster for the ceilings.

Over the years there have been some alterations and extensions to the original building, the first of these in 1951/52. Carried out by T.B. O'Meara & Sons, this work involved the partial removal of the verandahs, the construction of two new wings and extension of the main roof. The front verandah and facade were significantly altered. Sadly, most of the wrought-iron balustrading removed when the verandahs were demolished, was discarded.

Further extensions made to the offices in 1965/66 saw the removal of remaining verandahs and the introduction of air-conditioning to some rooms. Two new rear wings were added. The floor area was increased by 75 per cent so, with the previous increase in 1951, there was a total increase of 160 per cent to the size of the original building.

The only parts of the original building still remaining in their true form are the front entry porch, the steps and the fence. Internal alterations were made in later years and the Council building today represents a mixture of early 1950s and mid-1960s design.

In recent years some consideration was given to restoration of the building to its original appearance but the idea was abandoned because the result would have provided less office space.

CHICKEN NECTAR

Cut *1 chicken* into serving-sized pieces and place in a casserole dish.

Mix *1 packet Dutch Curry and Rice soup mix* with *850 ml (1½ pint) can apricot or peach nectar*. Pour over chicken and *season* to taste. Cover pan, bake in 180°C (350°F) oven for 10 minutes. Turn oven down to 150°C (300°F) and cook until tender, about 1–1½ hours.

Serve with *jacket potatoes* and *green vegetables*.

Serves 4.

POLYNESIAN BAKED CHICKEN

Shirley MacKenzie demonstrates cooking on television each week for the Far North Queensland Electricity Board. This is one of her recipes.

Shake *1 kg (2 lb) chicken pieces* in a plasic bag with *½ cup flour, 1 teaspoon each salt and pepper*. Place chicken in a buttered casserole dish and brush with *3 tablespoons butter*, melted. Bake in an electric oven at 180°C (350°F) until cooked.

Now make the *sauce*.

In a saucepan, combine and bring to the boil, stirring constantly:
½ cup orange juice
1 tablespoon lemon juice
¼ cup brown sugar
2 teaspoons soy sauce
2 teaspoons cornflour
When thickened, add:
½ a pineapple, cubed
½ a pawpaw, cubed
green capsicum, cut in strips
Pour over chicken and bake a further 10 minutes. Serve garnished with *sesame seeds*.

Serves 4.

AVOCADO CHICKEN BREASTS

Saute *3 chopped shallots* and *1 clove crushed garlic* in *3 tablespoons butter* for 1 minute. Add *250 g (8 oz) chopped green prawns* and a *chopped avocado*, cook slightly, then add *2 tablespoons each brandy and dry vermouth*.

Stir in *2 tablespoons flour* and *½ cup cream* and mix until a smooth sauce has formed. Season well with *salt and pepper* and allow to cool.

Flatten *six chicken breast fillets* and fill each with avocado mixture, then fold in half.

Brush one sheet of *filo pastry* with melted *butter*, place a second sheet on top, and brush with more butter. Fold pastry in half and place chicken breast into centre of pastry. Fold in the sides and roll up to form a parcel. Brush top with butter.

Repeat process with remaining chicken pieces — you will use 12 sheets of filo in all.

Place parcels onto a buttered baking tray and bake in a 180°C (350°F) oven for 30 minutes, or until golden brown.

Serves 6.

MARLIN COAST CHICKEN SALAD SUPREME

Combine in a bowl and chill for one hour:
4 cups diced, cooked chicken
1 cup celery, finely chopped
2 shallots, chopped
1 tablespoon capers
salt to taste
1 tablespoon lemon juice
Add:
1 can mandarin segments
1 x 440 g (15 oz) can pineapple pieces
Mix together *1 cup good home-made mayonnaise* with the grated *rind of 1 lemon*, and gently stir into the chicken. Top with *60 g (2 oz) toasted slivered almonds*.

This looks very attractive served in a clam shell.

Serves 8.

HONEY-SOY CHICKEN WINGS

Heat *2 tablespoons olive oil* in a wok and fry *1 kg (2 lb) chicken wings* at high heat for 5 minutes or until brown.

Add:
⅓ cup soy sauce
2 tablespoons honey
2 tablespoons green ginger wine
1 clove garlic, crushed
½ teaspoon grated green ginger

Reduce heat to low, cover and simmer about 30 minutes or until wings are tender. Stir frequently to ensure sweet glaze does not burn.

Serve with *rice* or as an appetiser.

Serves 5–6.

TROPICAL DUCKLING

Place a *2 kg (4 lb) duckling* in an ovenproof dish, sprinkle with *1 teaspoon mixed herbs*, and put *1 cup water* in dish. Cover with *foil* and bake in a very hot oven 250°C (500°F) for 1 hour.

Sauce
Combine in a saucepan and cook through:
1 kg (2 lb) sultana grapes
250 g (8 oz) chopped pawpaw
100 g (3 oz) sliced firm bananas
1½ cups milk
¾ cup cream
½ cup dry white wine

Thicken with some *cornflour* blended with a little *water*, just before boiling. Bring to boil and let simmer for 2 minutes.

Divide duckling into quarters and keep warm until ready to serve, then pour sauce over duckling.

Serves 4.

* V·E·G·E·T·A·B·L·E·S *

Here you'll find deliciously different ways of preparing common vegetables.

QUEENSLAND BLUE MICROWAVE

Cut the top off a *medium Queensland blue pumpkin* to make a lid. Scoop out seeds and fibres.

Mix together and spread inside pumpkin:

2 tablespoons honey
2 tablespoons melted butter
1 teaspoon nutmeg
pinch salt
ground pepper

Place pumpkin lid on and bake in a microwave for 8–10 minutes per 500 g (1 lb).

Serves 8.

SWEET AND SOUR CABBAGE

Place *2 tablespoons water* and *1 dessertspoon butter* in a saucepan and add:

¼ cabbage, chopped finely
1 green apple, grated
1 teaspoon sugar
1 small onion, chopped
1 teaspoon vinegar
small amount salt and pepper

Cook over low heat until tender.

Serves 6.

STUFFED EGGPLANT

Boil 4 *small eggplant* until tender, drain and while still warm cut in half lengthwise and scoop out all the pulp without damaging the skins.

Cut the crusts off 4 *slices bread*, boil bread in ½ *cup milk* and add to the eggplant pulp, mashing well. Add:

2 *eggs*
½ *cup grated romano cheese*

Chop up tomatoes from a 250 *g (8 oz) tin*, and place in a large flat dish with 2 *tablespoons oil or butter*, 1 *clove garlic*, chopped, and 1 *teaspoon salt*. Cook in hot oven 200°C (400°F) for 10 minutes.

Fill the eggplant skins with cheese mixture and place on tomato bed. Return to oven with a sheet of foil covering and cook for a further 30 minutes. Towards the end of cooking time, remove foil so the tops will brown.

Serves 4.

BAKED EGGPLANT

Peel and dice 1 *eggplant*. Cook in a little *water*.

Make a white sauce:
In a saucepan melt 2 *tablespoons butter*, off heat stir in 2 *tablespoons flour* and return to heat, stirring just until it bubbles. Off heat stir in gradually ⅔ *cup milk*, then bring to boil, stirring continuously.

Add 1 *cup cheese*, grated.

Drain and mash eggplant and add:
1 *cup breadcrumbs*
1 *cup tomatoes*
2 *egg yolks*, beaten
pinch salt

Mix into the white sauce, then fold in 2 *beaten egg whites*. Pour into greased casserole dish. Bake at 180°C (350°F) for 30 minutes.

Serves 4.

MACADAMIA BUTTERNUT PUMPKIN

Cut the tops off 3 *small butternut pumpkins* and reserve. Scoop out seeds and filaments and season with *salt and pepper.*

Melt 2 *tablespoons butter* and cook *½ cup sliced onions* until soft. Mix with:

½ cup chopped macadamia nuts, toasted
½ cup grated cheese
¼ cup sultanas
salt and pepper
½ teaspoon grated cardamon
1 egg
½ cup breadcrumbs

Fill pumpkins with this mixture and pour *⅓ cup cream into each.* Replace top of pumpkin and bake in a moderate oven 180°C (350°F) for 1 hour until pumpkin is tender and soft on the outside, and the inside is bubbling.

Cut into thick wedges and serve.

Serves 6–8.

WHOLE BAKED POTATOES

Scrub *potatoes* and rub over with *oil* and bake at 200°C (400°F) until tender, about 50–60 minutes. Allow to cool a little, then scoop out pulp, leaving hollowed-out shell.

Mix together in a bowl:

potato pulp
1 tablespoon grated cheese for each potato
salt and pepper
a little milk

Replace mashed pulp into skins and sprinkle with *extra grated cheese* and place under griller until browned.

KURANDA RAILWAY

Early Sunday morning and Cairns Railway Station is crowded with tourists waiting for the 8.30 am departure for Kuranda. This 'village in the rainforest' is an hour and a half away and the trip is a must for visitors to the North.

The Kuranda Railway stands as one of Australia's most amazing engineering feats. The successful tenderer for the job was John Robb, and the formidable task was begun in 1886, with picks and shovels the main implements. By the time the line was completed in 1891 35 men had lost their lives as a result of accidents and tropical diseases. At one stage more than a thousand men worked on the line, which rises 330 metres, has fifteen tunnels and ninety-eight curves. All steel bridging was riveted, as welding was unknown in those days, and some of the wooden bridges were built over ravines hundreds of metres deep.

Railway workers were given some respite from toil with the establishment of a township at Stoney Creek. This mountainous spot had sly grog shanties, amusement halls and even a Methodist Church. Michael Boland, who was later to build Boland's Store in Cairns, is believed to have owned his own small hotel at Stoney Creek — an enterprising young man!

Kuranda station at the end of the line must rate as one of the prettiest anywhere. Travellers are greeted by a plethora of greenery, with fern baskets hanging everywhere and plants to trip over. A few minutes' walk finds a modern shopping complex, a great restaurant called 'Frogs', an open marketplace providing an endless variety of home produce and Heritage Homestead which houses the 'Grubstake' restaurant. Built of local redgum, the building also houses a fine museum displaying replicas of shanty-town life in the early days.

The Kuranda railway is one of the north's greatest tourist attractions and looks set to stay that way!

VEGETABLE CUSTARD

1 egg
300 ml (½ pint) milk
1 medium carrot, diced
250 g (½ lb) peas or beans
1 tomato

Cook peas or beans and diced carrots until tender. Place in bottom of greased fireproof dish. Slice tomatoes on top. Beat egg, add milk and season. Pour over vegetables and cook in moderate oven 180°C (350°F) standing in water, until set, about½ hour.

Serves 3.

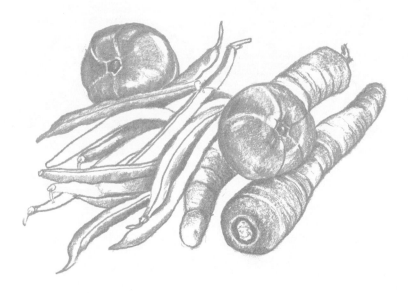

* S·A·L·A·D·S *

The exciting variety of fresh produce available in the Cairns district is reflected by the use of many fruits, vegetables and seafoods in this section.

NAUTILUS PRAWNS AND ZUCCHINI SALAD

For this, Mogens Bay Esbensen uses locally available *large leader prawns or tiger prawns.*

Peel and devein *8–12 prawns*, leaving the tails on, butterfly them and place on an oiled, seasoned ovenproof dish.

Slice *4 zucchini* lengthwise using a vegetable peeler, and blanch in boiling *water* for one minute. Strain and transfer zucchini to a dish. Sprinkle with *1 tablespoon tarragon vinegar*, season with *salt and pepper* and top with *1 shallot*, finely chopped.

Meanwhile, brush the prawns with *4 tablespoons Provencale oil spiced with pimento* and bake in a very hot oven 230°C (450°F) for 4 minutes. Remove to rest.

To serve, arrange the zucchini in a fan shape on a warm entree plate, place two or three prawns alongside, sprinkle with *vinegar* and chopped *fresh herbs*.

Serves 4–6.

HOUSE ON THE HILL

While much altered from its original construction, the House on the Hill remains a famous historical building.

Prominently situated on Ah Chung's Hill, it was built of cedar and hardwood in 1896 by Louis Severin for Richard Ash Kingsford, the first mayor of Cairns in 1895. Kingsford named the house 'Fairview'. It was bungalow style and the top of the hill had to be flattened to accommodate it.

Kingsford's eldest daughter, Catherine, married William Charles Smith, manager of the Cairns branch of the Bank of New South Wales. Their children retained the Kingsford name, and Charles Kingsford-Smith, their fourth son, went on to become a world famous aviator. 'Smithy' was hailed as an exceptionally brilliant pilot and navigator and when he and Ulm arrived at Cairns in 1932 after their daring round-Australia flight in the *Southern Cross* he was given a rousing welcome as grandson of R. A. Kingsford.

'Smithy' spent some of his childhood in Fairview, but of even greater historical significance was its use during World War II by the Australian Army as a secret headquarters and training camp for the Inter-Allied Services Branch, under the command of Major Trappes Lomax. From this house plans were made for raids behind enemy lines, and it was here also that the famous 'Z squad' commandoes trained for Operation Jaywick in 1943. Probably the greatest sea raid of the war, this involved sailing the *Krait*, a small motor vessel, to Singapore and back. Disguised as a fishing vessel it was responsible for the destruction of forty thousand tonnes of Japanese shipping in Singapore Harbour.

Known to the Army as Z.E.S. — Z. Experimental Station — the name 'Fairview' ceased to be used and now it is officially recognised as 'The House on the Hill'.

The house lay sadly neglected for many years until 1965 when it was extensively altered for use as a restaurant. In 1986, the House on the Hill operates as a nightclub restaurant.

ROCKMELON AND BANANA SALAD

This is a great favourite with *House on the Hill* patrons.
Combine in a bowl:
1 ripe rockmelon peeled, seeded and cubed
5 firm, ripe bananas peeled and sliced
Sprinkle over *juice of 1 lemon* to prevent discolouration.
Mix in gently:
300 g (10 oz) sour cream
1 dessertspoon honey
½ cup desiccated coconut
½ cup chopped unsalted peanuts
Serves 6.

ROGER'S CURRIED CHICKEN AND PECAN SALAD

In this recipe Dale Rogers utilises pecan nuts grown on the family
farm on the Atherton Tablelands.
Saute *1 small chopped onion* with *1 teaspoon of good curry powder*
and *1 teaspoon of butter*. Cool, and mix with:
1 cup pecan halves
2 cups diced cooked chicken pieces
2 cups diced celery
2 cups diced red-skinned apple
½ cup chopped parsley
Just before serving, mix through *½ cup sour cream* and adjust
seasoning.
Serves 4.

WATERMELON SALAD

Toss together and chill:
1 watermelon, cubed
1 medium onion, cut in thin rings
1 dessertspoon sugar
1 tablespoon vinegar
1 tablespoon olive oil
salt and pepper

POTATO AND PAWPAW SALAD

Firstly, make the *mango chutney dressing.*

Combine in a food processor and process until well combined:
1 *mild green chilli,* seeds removed and flesh roughly chopped
½ *cup oil*
2 *tablespoons vinegar*
2 *tablespoons mango chutney*
1 *teaspoon French mustard*
200 g (6 oz) *natural yoghurt*
dash tabasco sauce
salt and pepper to taste

Now, for the *salad.*

Cook 500 g (1 lb) *potatoes,* peeled, until tender then roughly chop.
Blanch 250 g (8 oz) *broccoli flowerettes.*

Combine potatoes with mango chutney dressing. Cover and chill.

Peel 1 *medium pawpaw,* remove seeds and cut into chunks.

Roll 8 *slices of ham* into cylinders.

To assemble:

Drain potatoes and reserve dressing. Arrange potatoes, broccoli, 1 *sliced cucumber,* 6 *chopped shallots,* and the pawpaw attractively in a salad bowl. Garnish with rolled ham. Serve with the reserved mango chutney dressing.

Serves 4–6.

BROAD BEAN SALAD

Remove ½–1 kg (1–2 lb) *beans* from their pods and cook until just tender. (You can also cook up with the beans, several of the younger tender pod skins. These can be chopped up and added to the salad.)

Add and toss together:
1–2 *tablespoons fennel or dill*
1 *clove crushed garlic*
2 *tablespoons olive oil*
2 *tablespoons lemon juice*
salt and freshly ground pepper
chopped shallots
chopped parsley

Serves 6.

SMOKED SALMON AND MELON SALAD

Chop 250 g (8 oz) smoked salmon into squares and keep chilled.
In a bowl combine:
2 cups honeydew melon, chopped
2 cups watermelon, chopped
½ cup grapefruit segments
2 cups rockmelon, chopped
Cover and keep chilled.
Just before serving, add the salmon to the melon with:
juice of 1 lemon
1 tablespoon fresh orange juice
1½ tablespoons olive oil
salt and fresh black pepper
Season slightly with salt and generously with pepper. Toss and
serve.
Serves 6.

A Cairns Resident

Rolfe Gelling grew up in Cairns, his family having moved from
Charters Towers with the advent of the gold slump. His father,
Richard Gelling, was coachbuilder in a family business and in
early 1904 was sent to Townsville, then by ship to Cairns to
report on the possibility of setting up a business there.

Having reported favourably, Richard and his brother Philip
came to Cairns to set up a business in 1905. Situated next to the
present ambulance building, the premises called Gelling Brothers
Pty Ltd consisted of a blacksmith shop and adjacent coach-
building shop. Their home stood alongside.

One of four children born to Richard and May Gelling, Rolfe, the
only son, was given his mother's maiden name. He too eventually
went into the family business after secondary schooling in
Townsville and two years with Burns Philp. He married a local girl
and when the business closed in 1948 Rolfe Gelling worked in
insurance until his retirement.

It is understandable that the coaching business never reached a
substantial size because most horse-drawn carriages had been
replaced by motor vehicles by the 1930s. When Rolfe was a small
boy he recalls only two car owners in Cairns.

During his secondary school days in Townsville Rolfe travelled back and forth by ship at holiday time. On one occasion when he was due to return to Townsville Grammar there was a shipping strike. The manager of the Adelaide Steamship Co. phoned Rolfe's father and offered a berth for his son and a schoolfriend on the company's ship *Caroo*. It was travelling from Port Douglas to Cairns to pick up sugar and passengers for Townsville at five pounds a head. On the Wednesday afternoon at 3 pm the boys boarded ship, which lifted anchor and moved off. The skipper refused to travel after dark so *Caroo* anchored off Fitzroy Island. Next day *Caroo* reached Mourylyan Harbour and stood off overnight. On Friday morning it ran aground on a mudbank in Hinchinbrook Passage where it spent Friday night.

Thirty-five fed-up passengers disembarked at Lucinda Harbour and the rest set out on Saturday morning, reaching Townsville entrance at 9 pm on Saturday night.

Rolfe and his friend thankfully left the ship and boarded a four-horse cab to go to school. A mile from school the cab lost a wheel so the two boys picked up their suitcases and walked to Townsville Grammar, arriving at 11 pm. 'Today', he says, 'Children go from Cairns to Townsville in thirty-five minutes.'

Some of Rolfe Gelling's most vivid memories relate to World War II as it affected Cairns residents. He remembers listening to radio broadcasts by Tokyo Rose, Lord Haw-Haw, Goebbels and Hitler, and recalls the Coral Sea Battle announcement when civilians waited to be called up, and the relief and joy when the Americans arrived.

Rolfe Gelling is a talented artist and has exhibited regularly. He served a term as council alderman — his father served several terms, with one as mayor. (It was Mayor Gelling who was responsible for changing the name of Sachs Street to Grafton Street.)

Mr and Mrs Rolfe Gelling thoroughly enjoy Cairns life and can think of no place they would prefer to be.

PLANTAINS

What are they? They are a type of banana used extensively in the West Indies and Pacific Islands as a vegetable. Plantains are a most versatile fruit or vegetable, depending on how they are served. Here are some suggestions from The Berrys of High Falls Farm.

With salads:

Serve 3 or 4 thin slices with meat and/or vegetable salads. Fruit must be fully mature, that is, about equivalent to an over-ripe ordinary banana.

Fruit salad:

Use in the normal way. Fruit must be fully mature.

Grilled or barbecued:

Cook thin slices until tender and serve as a substitute for eggs. Equally as tasty with fish, chicken, steak or pork. Fruit can be used at any stage of ripening.

Boiled or baked:

Cook in a similar manner to potatoes. Fruit should be green but fully developed. To peel a green banana or plantain remove ends, cut lengthwise on each corner and peel each section.

As a dessert:

Fry lightly and serve with cream or ice-cream. A dash of rum or brandy is an optional extra. Plantains make excellent fritters.

These are the normal uses of the plantain. Exotic recipe books offer many variations of uses.

Plantains keep much better than ordinary bananas and when fully ripened may be kept under normal household refrigeration. The skins may go black but the fruit retains its quality.

AVOCADO MAYONNAISE

Mix together and beat well:
2 tablespoons evaporated milk
1 tablespoon lemon juice
1 teaspoon prepared mustard
¾ cup mashed avocado

Season to taste with *paprika, salt* and *tabasco sauce*.

* D·E·S·S·E·R·T·S *

Just the mention of tropical fruits conjures up thoughts of irresistible culinary delights — these recipes fall into that category.

PAWPAW SOUFFLE

Heat together until boiling:
2 cups mashed pawpaw
½ cup water
½ cup sugar
Mix 30 g (1 oz) arrowroot or cornflour with ½ cup lemon juice and add to pawpaw. Stir over heat until it thickens. Add the yolks of 2 eggs, beaten.
When nearly cold, carefully fold 2 stiffly beaten egg whites into the mixture.
Serve cold.
Serves 4–6.

FRESH PEACH PIE

Peel 6 medium-sized peaches and cut in halves. Place in a 24 cm (9 in) unbaked pastry shell, cut side up.
Mix together and pour over peaches:
1 cup sugar
2 tablespoons melted butter
2 beaten eggs
Bake for 10 minutes at 210°C (425°F), then at 180°C (350°F) for a futher 20 minutes. Serve warm or cold.
Serves 8.

MANGO CREAM PIE

Crumb crust
Combine 125 g (4 oz) plain sweet biscuits, finely crushed, and 60 g (2 oz) melted butter. Press into a springform pan or pie plate.

Filling
Mash 2 ripe mangoes to give 1–1¼ cups pulp. Add 1 *dessertspoon lemon juice* and ¼ *cup sugar*.

Sprinkle 1 *dessertspoon gelatine* over 1 *tablespoon cold water*, stand to soften then dissolve over hot water. Add to mango mixture.

Beat 150 ml (¼ pint) cream until firm, and fold lightly into mango mixture. Spread into pie crust and refrigerate until firm.

Decorate with *extra whipped cream* and *passionfruit*.

Serves 6.

Note: Canned mango may be used — drain well and omit sugar. This mixture may also be pressed into a slab tin (lined with foil) and cut into squares for easy serving.

ORANGE AND MANGO PIE

Make a biscuit base by combining 250 g (8 oz) *crushed plain sweet biscuits* with 125 g (4 oz) *melted butter*. Press over the base and sides of a 20 cm (8 in) springform pan. Refrigerate while preparing filling.

Filling
Puree 2 x 425 g (14 oz) *cans mango slices* and 1 *cup mango juice* from the slices in a food processor. Add ½ *teaspoon grated orange rind* and ⅓ *cup orange juice*.

Dissolve 1 *tablespoon gelatine* in ⅓ *cup water* and add to mango mixture. Process until well combined, then transfer to a large bowl. Fold through:
2 *egg whites*, softly beaten
300 ml (1½ cups) *cream*, whipped

Pour mixture into prepared biscuit crust. Refrigerate until set.

Decorate with *extra whipped cream* and *passionfruit pulp*.

Serves 8.

STEAMED RAISIN AND ORANGE PUDDING

This recipe has been adapted from one published in the *Cairns Post* in 1942.

Beat to a cream:
60 g (2 oz) butter
60 g (2 oz) sugar
Add *2 well-beaten eggs* and *grated rind of 1 orange*
Fold in:
150 g (5 oz) self-raising flour }
pinch salt } combined

Add *fresh orange juice* to make a soft dropping consistency (juice of half an orange is usually needed). Butter a pudding basin thickly, press most of 250 g (8 oz) raisins onto sides stirring remainder into mixture.

Pour into basin, cover with buttered paper and steam for 2 hours in boiling water covering half the depth of boiler.

Serve with *vanilla custard.*

Serves 6.

BRANDY PEACHES

Base
Place in a mixing bowl and beat till soft peaks form:
4 egg whites
½ teaspoon vanilla
½ teaspoon salt
¾ teaspoon cream of tartar
Gradually add *1⅓ cups caster sugar* and beat until sugar is dissolved. Place mixture on a foil-covered tray and bake in a very slow oven for 45 minutes. Then turn oven off and leave for a further 45 minutes to dry.

Filling
Drain a *825 g (1 lb 10 oz) can peach halves* and place peaches on top of base.
Mix together and heat over a double boiler till smooth:
2 tablespoons fresh orange juice
½ cup Grand Marnier
500 g (1 lb) cooking chocolate, melted
Pour over peaches on base and refrigerate until ready to serve.
Serve with *ice-cream or whipped cream.*
Serves 8–10.

McKENZIE HOUSE

This beautiful old house has had a timely facelift in recent years and on first sight it was a 'must' for me to draw. It sits proudly on the corner of Lake and McKenzie streets — that street named after a former mayor, C. J. McKenzie, who held office three times between 1905 and 1913.

The house was built about 1928 by a Mr Morgan who was the manager of White Car Coaches servicing the Atherton Tablelands. It was sold to Mrs Johnston in 1946, and she lived in the house until her death in 1975.

The Johnston family previously lived in a house adjacent to the Cairns Base Hospital. They were forced to move when the house was resumed for extensions to the hospital. The family was involved in sawmilling and ran a sawmill in the Stratford–Freshwater area.

Two Johnston children inherited the house. Mr Rex Johnston and his sister renovated it and rented it out while waiting for a buyer. Although the asking price was $50 000, it was eventually sold for $30 000 to Garth and Jeanette Gifford who lived there until 1981 when they sold it to John Bottoms and Graham Knell. McKenzie House, as the new owners named it, now contains the offices of Graham Knell and Co, Solicitors.

It is hard to imagine that the whole area was originally swampland, with a creek running through what is now the backyard of the house. In fact most of Cairns was built on similar land.

A neighbour recalls that the house was originally lower set and was beautifully furnished. A maple bedroom setting was apparently the prize attraction. Made by Cairns furniture makers, Svendens, it did indeed win a prize at the Cairns Show!

The present owners of McKenzie House have had it raised by about half a metre to facilitate future building underneath. Architect Bill Cuningham has designed office space for that area in keeping with the old-world character of the house.

Graham Knell and John Bottoms had to overcome strong council opposition to suburban spot development — and indeed it was reported in the press at the time that this was to be the last! Since then, quite a few old houses have been converted to business premises, all with the same emphasis on retention of character. As reported in the *Cairns Post*: 'Their elegant lines, old world charm and plain practicality are seducing new owners into recycling, renovating and refurbishing, rather than wrecking and rebuilding.'

NON DAIRY FOOD ICE-CREAM

In a blender put:
300 g (10 oz) *fresh strawberries or bananas, pawpaws, avocado or stewed prunes*
1 cup *peach, apricot or pear juice*
2 tablespoons *carob powder*
1 teaspoon *vanilla*
In a saucepan over very low heat melt:
100 g (3½ oz) *creamed coconut*
1 cup *fresh juice*, as above
Cool slightly, add to blender and blend at very high speed for several minutes.
Freeze in trays for 3–4 hours. Defrost a little before serving.
To serve, top with *fresh fruit salad* or layer ice-cream, fruit salad, and then ice-cream again.
Serves 6.

CHOCOLATE RUM CREAM DESSERT

In a saucepan put 125 g *(4 oz) dark cooking chocolate* and melt over hot water. Set aside.
Soften 2 *dessertspoons gelatine* in ¼ cup *cold water* then set over *hot water* to dissolve.
In a bowl beat 500 g *(1 lb) cream cheese* until smooth and blend in:
½ cup *milk*
1 cup *sugar*
dissolved gelatine
Pour 3 cups of this mixture into a bowl and beat in the melted chocolate.
Pour into a dish and refrigerate until set. To the remaining mixture add 3 *dessertspoons rum* then fold in 2 *cups cream*, whipped.
Spoon on top of set chocolate layer and refrigerate until set. Garnish with *grated chocolate*.
Serves 8.

MACADAMIA FUDGE TOPPING FOR ICE-CREAM

Melt *1½ tablespoons butter* and add *2 tablespoons each caster sugar and brown sugar*. Stir until sugar is dissolved.

Add and stir again:
1 tablespoon golden syrup
1 tablespoon cocoa

Add *½ cup cream* and simmer for 5 minutes. Add:
60 g (2 oz) macadamia nuts, roasted then chopped
½ teaspoon vanilla

Mix thoroughly and spoon over ice-cream.

Serves 4–6.

INGRAM'S ICE-CREAM

Pureed fresh fruit and cream form the basis for this delicious natural food made by Jim and Irene Ingram at their Port Douglas wharfside shop.

While the Ingrams use ice-cream machines, it can be made in the refrigerator as long as the mixture is softened and beaten twice and refrozen before serving.

Here's the recipe using bananas — fruit of your choice may be substituted.

Puree *8–10 bananas* and blend with:
1 cup lemon juice
½ cup sugar syrup made with raw sugar (optional)

Add *2 cups thick whipping cream*, put in ice-cream machine and churn for 15 minutes.

Makes 12 serving cups.

ZABAGLIONE

Beat *6 egg yolks* with *6 level tablespoons sugar* in an electric mixer until frothy, and continue beating while slowly adding *6 tablespoons medium sherry*.

Pour into a saucepan and cook in a double boiler while stirring continuously with a wooden spoon till mixture falls off spoon when tapped on the edge of a saucepan.

Pour into individual serving dishes and serve with a wafer biscuit.

May be eaten hot or cold.

Serves 6.

TROPICAL TRIFLE

Cut a *sponge sandwich* into cubes and arrange half on the base of an ovenware dish.

Blend *2 tablespoons cornflour* with *a little milk from 1¾ cups* and add to the remainder of the milk with *2 tablespoons sugar*. Stir until boiling, and simmer for 3 minutes. Cool slightly.

Add *2 beaten egg yolks*. Cook a few minutes over low heat without boiling. Add *1 dessertspoon sherry*.

Pour half over the cake in dish. Cover with *¾ cup finely chopped cooked pineapple*, drained, then add remaining cake cubes, a layer of custard then *another ¾ cup pineapple*.

Make a meringue with *2 egg whites* and *4 tablespoons sugar*, and pile around the edge of the dish. Place in oven until light brown. Allow to get cold then chill.

Fill the centre with chopped *red jelly* and decorate with chopped *blanched almonds* and *strawberries*.

Whipped cream can be substituted for the meringue if preferred.

Serves 8–10.

MONA'S TROPICAL PUDDING

Sift together:
1 cup plain flour
1 cup sugar
1 teaspoon bicarbonate of soda
¼ teaspoon salt
Add:
2 cups canned or fresh fruit salad
1 egg
1 teaspoon vanilla

Put in a baking dish, cover with *½ cup brown sugar* and *½ cup walnuts*.

Bake at 180°C (350°F) for 30 minutes.

Serves 6.

* C·A·K·E·S & C·O *

Even in this section fruits feature prominently and you'll find some old timers as well as exciting newer recipes.

GRAMMA PUMPKIN CAKE

Beat together *1 cup sugar* and *185 g (6 oz) butter*. Add *2 eggs* and beat again, then fold in:
1 cup cooked pumpkin (gramma)
1 x 375 g (12 oz) packet mixed fruit
2½ cups self-raising flour
1 tablespoon golden syrup
lemon essence
Bake in a moderate oven 180°C (350°F) for 1 to 1¼ hours. Ice with *lemon icing*.

BANANA AND WALNUT CAKE

Cream *125 g (4 oz) butter* with *¾ cup caster sugar* until light and fluffy. Add *2 eggs*, one at a time, beating well after each addition. Add *¾ cup mashed, very ripe bananas* and *1 teaspoon vanilla*, and beat on low speed until well combined. Stir in *½ cup chopped walnuts* then:
¾ cup self-raising flour
¾ cup plain flour   } sifted together
1 teaspoon bicarbonate of soda
Spread mixture into well-greased 20 cm (8 in) ring tin and bake in a moderate oven 180°C (350°F) for 40 minutes, or until cooked when tested.

One of north
Queensland's most
attractive old
buildings, Bolands
was completely
renovated in
1985.

As Bolands Pty. Ltd.
and later, David
Jones, it was
a success story of
the north, and
saw nearly a
century of drive
by the Boland
family.

BOLAND'S STORE

Michael Boland was only eighteen years old when as an Irish immigrant he arrived alone in Melbourne in 1881. With a half crown in his pocket, an adventurous spirit and keen business sense, this young man found his way to Cairns a year later.

The Kuranda Railway was under construction, and as the line progressed, so too with the help of a packhorse did a small tentful of provisions supplied by Boland for the workers. Michael Boland is also credited with ownership of a small hotel at Stoney Creek, Barron Falls.

He worked in manual jobs for a few years and by 1887 had saved enough money to open a small business — 'M. Boland General Merchant' — in Abbott Street. In 1900 he moved the business to Spence Street.

Michael Boland nurtured a dream of building his own special store and to achieve this end commissioned an architect, E. Gregory Waters, to design a suitable building. While Cairns residents were sceptical there was no doubt in Boland's mind that his dream would be realised. The builder was a Mr Bulcock. The steelwork was done by Dorman Long and Co, English shipbuilders and engineers. It was prefabricated in England, shipped to Cairns and bolted together on site. The walls were made of concrete based on imported cement.

The fine three-storeyed store on the corner of Lake and Spence streets was commenced in 1911 and completed in 1914 — just prior to the beginning of World War I. Because of the war, building costs escalated from the estimated twelve to thirteen thousand pounds to eighteen thousand pounds.

Bolands Pty Ltd became a success story of the north, due largely to the business acumen of its founder. Michael Boland ran the business for twenty-six years, until his death in 1923 when Cairns lost one of its most public spirited citizens.

Thomas, the youngest of three sons, then managed the business until 1963 when it was sold to David Jones. Thomas retired the same year and in 1964 his son Terry was appointed manager — almost a century of service by the Boland family.

In 1984 Townsville-based developers, Kern Corporations, bought the building and by mid-1985 had completed renovations. Retaining the original facade, the interior contains an exciting new retail complex, junior department store, national specialty retailers, Statewide Building Society and fine food court. All that — and modern air-conditioned commercial premises above.

PASSIONFRUIT BUTTER BOLAND

This recipe was contributed by Eileen Fisk, Michael Boland's grand-daughter. Her other contributions can be located through the index.

Beat 3 eggs (at room temperature) with 250 g (8 oz) sugar in a saucepan. Add:

pulp of 8 passionfruit
3 tablespoons lemon juice
60 g (2 oz) butter

Bring slowly to the boil, stirring constantly. Simmer for 15 minutes, stirring occasionally. Allow to cool before bottling. Stir well again before bottling.

Boland's Store
In the early days of Boland's Store, a huge Christmas cake used
to be displayed in the window, containing a large sum of money
in sovereigns, half sovereigns and silver coins. Each customer was
given a small piece of cake in a container and the lucky ones found
and kept the coins inside their cake.

PAWPAW SCONES

Peel *1 small ripe pawpaw*, remove seeds and roughly chop flesh.
Place in a saucepan and gently cook until flesh becomes soft and
mushy. Do not add any water. Drain away any excess liquid.
Measure out ½ cup pawpaw flesh.

Cream together *2 tablespoons butter* with *¼ cup caster sugar*. Add
1 beaten egg and pawpaw and mix well.

Add alternately with *¾ cup milk* until smooth dough is formed:
2½ cups self-raising flour
1 teaspoon salt
¼ teaspoon nutmeg } mixed together
¼ teaspoon cinnamon

Knead gently on a lightly floured board. Cut scones with a 2.5 cm
(1 in) cutter. Brush with *topping* and bake on a buttered baking
tray at 200°C (400°F) for 12–15 minutes. *Or*, place scones on a
trivet in a preheated electric frypan. Cook for 20 minutes with lid
on and vent open.

Topping
Combine *1 tablespoon melted butter* with *¼ teaspoon each of nutmeg*
and cinnamon.

WARTIME ECONOMY RECIPE
HOW TO MAKE SAVOURY SCONES

Sift:
2 cups Simon's self-raising flour
½ teaspoon salt

Work in *1 tablespoon butter*. Add *¾ cup milk* to make soft dough.
Roll about ¼ inch (1 cm) thick. Cut into 3 inch (7½ cm) circles.
Spread with a *savoury paste* and fold over, pressing edges together.
Brush tops with *milk*. Bake in a hot oven 450°F (220°C) for 12
minutes. Serve hot, split and buttered.
Makes 12.

MANGO BREAD

Sift together:
2 cups flour
2 teaspoons cinnamon
2 teaspoons baking powder
½ teaspoon salt
Make a well in dry ingredients and add:
3 eggs
1 teaspoon vanilla
¾ cup cooking oil
1¼ cups sugar
¼ cup walnuts
½ cup coconut
2 cups diced mango
Mix well and place into well-greased loaf tin. Let stand for 20 minutes before baking at 180°C (350°F) for 1 hour.

COCONUT DELIGHTS

Place in a bowl:
1 cup self-raising flour
1 cup cornflakes
1 cup desiccated coconut
1 cup sugar
1 tablespoon cocoa
Melt 125 g (4 oz) butter with 1 dessertspoon golden syrup and 1 tablespoon milk. Add to dry ingredients and mix well.

Put into a greased tray 18 cm x 27 cm (7 in x 11 in) and press down firmly. Bake in a moderately slow oven 160°C (325°F) about 20 minutes. Don't overcook or the slice will be too crisp.

Ice with chocolate icing as soon as it comes from the oven. Cut into squares.

FRESHWATER CONNECTION

My first reaction to this relatively new complex was utter astonishment that one man's vision could have created such an exciting attraction.

The Freshwater Connection is an embarking point for the Kuranda rail trip and less than a ten-minute drive from Cairns. Looking across the sugarcane fields, it is an idyllic spot.

The little village of Freshwater has seen much activity at the station. Not only were three 1908 rail carriages restored and positioned on either side of the platform, but the platform itself was tiled and converted to a delightful Raffles-style dining area. Tables and chairs are screened by lush potted palms; ferns and globe lights swing from tall poles supporting the most elaborate trussed roof. The whole appearance is one of breathtaking delight.

Carriage diners enjoy good food in private compartments, in an old-world atmosphere created by authentic restoration. Original lighting, fans, windows, seats, ceilings and iron mesh luggage racks have all been restored. The rail carriages can cater for a hundred diners and the platform settings provide for another hundred and twenty. At the latter, visitors are welcome to take light meals during the day. Opened in 1984, Freshwater Connection is the biggest family restaurant north of Brisbane.

Adjacent to the dining area is the main administration area containing a briefing area for Kuranda passengers, rest area and shop.

In lush surroundings it represents a step back into history, to a time when the rail-line to Kuranda was under construction; when picks and shovels were the main tools used to carve a track up the sides of the Barron Gorge; when great feats of engineering resulted in tunnels and bridges being constructed over a five-year period to reach Kuranda, now a one and half hour train journey from Cairns.

CARROT FRUIT CAKE

This cake freezes well.

Beat together *90 g (3 oz) butter* with *¾ cup sugar*, then add *2 eggs*, one at a time, beating well after each addition.

Sift together and beat into creamed mixture with *¼ cup milk*:
1¼ cups self-raising flour
pinch salt
¼ teaspoon bicarbonate of soda
½ teaspoon cinnamon

Stir in:
½ cup grated carrot
¼ cup glace cherries
¼ cup raisins
2 tablespoons chopped, blanched almonds

Spoon into a well-greased large loaf tin and bake in a moderate oven 180°C (350°F) for 50 to 60 minutes or until firm to touch and quite brown.

COCONUT CAKE

Place *1 cup desiccated coconut* in a bowl and pour over *1 cup boiling milk*. Let stand for 10 minutes then drain mixture through fine sieve. Retain ¼ cup of the liquid for the cake. Discard the remaining milk, but retain coconut.

Beat *3 egg whites* until stiff peaks form. Gradually add *½ cup caster sugar*, beating well between each addition. Stir in coconut.

With a handbeater, cream together *125 g (4 oz) butter* with *½ cup caster sugar* until soft and fluffy. Add *3 egg yolks*, one at a time, then *1 teaspoon vanilla essence*. Fold in *1 cup self-raising flour*, and the reserved *¼ cup coconut milk*.

Pour batter into a buttered 20 cm (8 in) springform pan. Spread with the coconut meringue mixture and bake in a 180°C (350°F) oven for 40 minutes.

The meringue will be quite brown but turn the oven down if colouring too quickly.

TROPICAL MANGO CHEESECAKE

This was a great favourite of the late Bob Dyer, a frequent visitor to Cairns.

Crust

Make a crumb crust using *375 g (12 oz) plain sweet biscuits*, crushed, and *185 g (6 oz) melted butter*. Press into a greased 24 cm (9 in) springform tin. Refrigerate for 1 hour.

Filling

In a food processor place:

1½ tablespoons gelatine
1 tablespoon lemon juice
grated rind of 1 lemon
½ cup hot water

Blend on high speed for about 40 seconds. Add:

⅓ cup sugar
3 egg yolks
250 g (8 oz) cream cheese
500g (1 lb) mango pulp

Blend for a further 20 seconds. Add:

375 g (12 oz) mango pulp
3 tablespoons iced water
300 ml (½ pint) sour cream

Blend until all are well combined.

Pour the mixture into the prepared crumb crust and refrigerate until set.

To serve, spread another *125 g (4 oz) mango pulp* over the top of the cheesecake and top with whipped *cream*.

Serves 10–12.

LEMON COOKIES

Cream *150 g (5 oz) butter* with *¾ cup sugar* until light and fluffy. Add *2 eggs* and *2 teaspoons grated lemon rind* and beat well.

Fold in *2 cups sifted self-raising flour* and mix well. Drop teaspoonfuls of mixture into *2 cups rice bubbles*. Roll lightly.

Place on a lightly greased oven tray and bake in a moderately hot oven 10–12 minutes.

Makes about 40 biscuits.

THE CAIRNS POST

The *Cairns Post* newspaper celebrated its hundredth birthday in 1982, and the calm facade of its impressive building has hidden seemingly endless frenzied activity over the years.

The first edition of the *Cairns Post* hit the streets on 10 May 1883, and a year later it was issued every Thursday for the princely sum of two pence. Proprietors were Messrs Wimble and Wall. Fred J. Wimble is credited with having founded the newspaper, published originally from timber premises in Lake Street.

The year 1882 is recorded on the present building because that marked the appearance of Cairns' first news-sheet, produced weekly by Mr E. Toft and his sister. They called it the *Cairns Telegraph* and the original issue was a mere half page long. The *Cairns Post* had some competition between 1885 and 1888 from the *Cairns Chronicle* and later from the *Trinity Times* (1901–10).

After Fred J. Wimble came Henderson and Bates, who controlled the newspaper until 1895. Then the *Cairns Morning Post* appeared, owned and edited by E. C. M. ('Hoppy') Draper, previously editor of the *Chronicle*. This newspaper is regarded as being the most direct ancestor of the present publication. On 'Hoppy' Draper's death in 1901 it was taken over by his brother A. J. Draper, one of Cairns' most respected citizens. He was elected mayor of Cairns seven times, the last term in 1924 ending not long before his death in 1928.

When the graceful columned building was erected in 1908 the newspaper was issued twice weekly, consisted of four pages and cost one penny. Harvey Draper was the architect who designed the imposing building, and alterations made in 1926 kept to the original design. The Draper family owned and controlled the newspaper until 1965 when the company was purchased by Queensland Press Ltd.

In 1926 the *Cairns Post* ran from twelve to sixteen pages and had wide northern circulation. Since then it has developed in line with technological advances and the development of the city itself. The first teleprinter was installed in 1949 and communications have progressively improved since then.

To commemorate the *Cairns Post's* centenary, a special ninety-six page supplement was produced — itself an historical document — and editor Alan Hudson reiterated the newspaper's

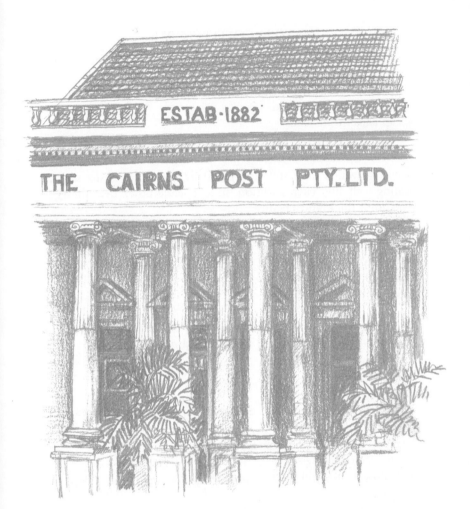

policy: 'This is to inform readers of events both at home and around the world, to advance Cairns and regional issues which we consider worthwhile and generally to continue to be a constructive element in our community.'

There is no doubting the value of the newspaper as an historical source. For my own purposes in preparing this book, past pages provided a fascinating insight into the everyday lives of community members, as well as a record of the region's growth and development.

FROZEN COFFEE TORTE

Combine and press into the base of a greased 20 cm (8 in) springform tin:

½ packet plain chocolate biscuits, crushed
60 g (2 oz) butter, melted
¼ cup chopped almonds
1½ tablespoons caster sugar

Dissolve 1 tablespoon instant coffee in 1 tablespoon hot water.

Beat 4 egg whites until stiff, and gradually add ½ cup caster sugar, beating well after each addition. In a separate bowl, beat the egg yolks until thick and creamy.

Whip a 300 ml (½ pint) jar of cream, fold in 1 tablespoon coffee liqueur or brandy, and add egg whites with coffee mixture and egg yolks.

Pour onto the prepared base, cover with foil and freeze. Serve frozen, cut into wedges.

Serves 8.

DATE AND GINGER BALLS

In a saucepan, mix together and slowly bring to a simmer:

250 g (8 oz) dates, chopped
100 g (3 oz) butter
½ cup sugar

Simmer for 6 minutes, take off heat and cool for 3 minutes.

Add to:

3 tablespoons chopped preserved ginger
2 cups rice bubbles

Roll into balls, roll balls in desiccated coconut and keep in refrigerator.

These balls are a handy standby for busy weeks.

Makes about 40.

PASSIONFRUIT CURD

Place 4 tablespoons butter and 1 cup sugar in a saucepan over heat and melt slowly.

Combine 6 passionfruit and 2 beaten eggs and stir into butter mixture. Simmer slowly until the mixture reaches the consistency of honey.

Pour into small jars.

* INDEX OF RECIPES *

(and recipe contributors)